Find your true identity through faith.

"I believe one of the surprises God gives us as a result of believing in Him and belonging to the household of faith is the gift of identity. Believing and belonging are two essential realities of the life of faith. To believe means to trust a personal God with your personal life and thus to enter into a dynamic and endless relationship with Him.

"Belonging follows belief. When we give our life to God, He gives us a family. ... Our loneliness and isolation are over. We are accepted and loved, warts and all, by the family of God.

"When we meet the King and become part of His family, we find out who we are, and life is never the same for us again. It is not easy to become a child of the King, but it is life's ultimate adventure."

BRUCE LARSON

BOOKS BY BRUCE LARSON:

Believe and Belong
There's a Lot More to Health Than Not Being Sick
Dare to Live Now
Living on the Growing Edge
No Longer Strangers
The One and Only You
Thirty Days to a New You
Risky Christianity
The Meaning and Mystery of Being Human
Setting Men Free
The Emerging Church
Ask Me to Dance

WITH KEITH MILLER:

The Edge of Adventure
Living the Adventure
The Passionate People: Carriers of the Spirit

Believe and Belong

Bruce Larson

Fleming H. Revell Company
Old Tappan, New Jersey

Scripture quotations identified KJV are from the King James Version of the Bible.

Scripture quotations identified RSV are from the Revised Standard Version of the Bible, copyrighted 1946, 1952, © 1971 and 1973.

Library of Congress Cataloging in Publication Data

Larson, Bruce.
  Believe and belong.

  1. Sermons, American. 2. Presbyterian Church—
Sermons. I. Title.
BX9178.L36B44   252'.051   81-23508
ISBN 0-8007-5087-X   AACR2

Contents

Preface

Believing and belonging are two essential realities of the life of faith. To believe means to trust a personal God with your personal life and thus to enter into a dynamic and endless relationship with Him. Belonging follows belief. When we give our life to God, He gives us a family. We suddenly belong, not only to the communion of the saints, but to a weird, peculiar group of Christians, our neighbors in the town where we live and believers all over the globe. Our loneliness and isolation are over. We are accepted and loved, warts and all, by the family of God.

The Bible underscores that this is what true faith is all about. But, of course, there is more—much more—involved in the pilgrim way. There is power and authority. There is peace and wisdom. There are gifts and by-products which the Bible calls "fruits." And there are all sorts of surprises.

Few things in life are as much fun as surprises. Do you remember as a child hearing the magic words from a visiting uncle or a friend of the family, "I have a surprise for you"? Then you were handed a mysterious package marvelously tied with a string or ribbon. Almost fifty years later I can still remember some of those unexpected gifts: an "official" Boy Scout hatchet (before I was old enough to be a scout); a flashlight with the choice of a red, green, or white beam; a collapsible drinking cup with a built-in compass. Even as adults those are magic moments when a spouse, one of your children, or a friend says, "Close your eyes. I have a surprise for you." The joy of a good surprise never seems to fade. We never outgrow it.

As Christians, we believe that we are made in God's image. Therefore it is only natural to assume that God must also love surprises. Maybe that is what G. K. Chesterton meant when he said that the trouble with God is that He is neither logical nor illogical, but almost logical. But what else! Someone who is almost logical is unpredictable and capable of surprises. Since God is the Author of joy, the Source of joy and the Giver of the gift of joy, certainly He must love to surprise us with good things and share our joy and delight.

One of God's best surprises is the one that comes as a result of believing and belonging. That surprising gift is the gift of identity. When I find God and become a part of His family, I suddenly discover who I am. I am *not* who my parents told me I was. I am *not* who my family and friends tell me I am. I am *not* who my culture and society tell me I am. As I believe and belong, I begin to find my true self.

It is a discovery of enormous value in living life day by day. If I know who I am, then all else falls into place. I know where I belong, where I am going, what companions and equipment I will need for the journey. Beyond that, I begin to understand what kind of work I am most suited for and what makes my moods go up and down. Identity is the philosopher's stone of the soul. I sought God for Himself, and He surprised me by revealing my true nature.

In a way, the best surprises are somewhat unpredictable. The nature of the giver and the nature of the recipient are revealed in the appropriateness of the gift. It is not so surprising to find that God is the answer to the eternal human riddle of "Who am I?" There is a delightful fable that comes from the Far East about an orphaned tiger cub. This poor little waif was adopted by a herd of kindly and compassionate goats, who raised him as one of their own. This meant that he ate grass like a goat, played like a goat, and even bleated like a goat. One day the king of the tigers came out of the jungle and entered the meadow where the goat family lived. All of the goats were terrified and ran for their lives, leaving the bewildered little tiger cub with the great king tiger. For some reason the cub felt unafraid. Then the king looked sternly at him and asked him what he was doing behaving like a goat. The cub didn't understand him for he had never learned tiger talk. He just bleated and looked puzzled. Then the king picked him up by the scuff of his neck, brought him over to a still pond and made him look at their reflections. At first the cub was puzzled and didn't understand. Then the king offered the cub his first piece of real tiger food. It was strange and he didn't like the smell and the taste of it. But he tried it anyway. As he ate more and more, something began to happen to him. His whole being began to change. Suddenly he let out a mighty roar that could be heard all over the jungle. At last he knew who he was. He had seen the king.

Well, that's what this book is about. When we meet the King and become part of His family, we find out who we are, and life is never the same for us again. It is not easy to become a child of the King, but it is life's ultimate adventure.

This book is a collection of sermons and talks written during the first year of my current pastorate at University Presbyterian Church in Seattle. I want to thank some of the people who are responsible for its existence. First there are the members of University Presbyterian Church who were, and continue to be, partners in dialogue. Next there is my beloved wife, Hazel, lifelong partner, friend, and editor, who has transformed a group of sermons into a book. Assisting in the process by encouraging and typing were my faithful secretary and friend Gretha Osterberg and my colleague and friend Hal Jaenson.

A Personal Word from the Editor
(and the Author's Wife)

Dear Reader:

I have been listening to Bruce, in private and public, for almost thirty years now. When I accompany him on speaking dates, I am often asked if I am not tired of hearing him. I always say quite honestly that he is my favorite preacher.

That's one reason why I am glad that God has called him back to a pastorate after a twenty-one-year absence. He has an opportunity to preach on a regular basis to a faithful congregation that includes me. I have found there is something especially exciting about hearing God speak a particular word to a particular group of people through a particular person on a continuing basis.

This book represents sermons from the first year of Bruce's pastorate at University Presbyterian Church in Seattle, Washington. In editing them for publication, I have

had a special problem. At first I thought I would attempt to
make them into more of a "book"—one in which there is a
sustained progression of thought and a less abrupt style. But
I decided instead that the sermons have a special value in
their present form.

I know that one of Bruce's choicest times each week
comes on his day off when he has an hour or so to read sermons that have been sent him by valued colleagues or
friends. Those particular sermons seem to bless him in a way
in which books do not. A sermon, a good one anyway, captures the now and the particular, the immediacy of God. I
was reluctant to tamper with that special quality, and I am
hoping that in reading this book you will feel it as well.
Books are not sermons and a sermon is not a book and there
is a place for each. In the last ten years, I have been helping
Bruce to write books. I have been thrilled to be a part of this
ministry. With the exception of chapters eleven and twelve,
which are drawn from material presented at a counseling
workshop, this book is a collection of sermons, and I hope
God will use it in many lives.

HAZEL LARSON

BELIEVE AND BELONG

1

Believing Begins with a Yes

A friend of mine is a professor at an Ivy League school. He told me about a conversation he overheard at a cocktail party he went to some time ago. The head of the astronomy department was speaking to the dean of the divinity school. The astronomy professor said, "Now, let's face it. In religion, what it all boils down to very simply is that you should love your neighbor as you love yourself. It's the Golden Rule, right?" "Yes, I suppose that's true," replied the dean of the divinity school. "Just as in astronomy it all boils down to one thing—'Twinkle, twinkle, little star'." I think we all have a tendency to want to make truth so simple that it's ridiculous. We can then say, "Well, if that's what it is, forget it."

Nevertheless, I would suggest to you that the essence of life consists largely of one simple truth: the art of knowing when to say yes and when to say no. These are the words that determine the direction and quality of our lives. You say yes or no to continuing your education. You say yes or no to a particular job. You say yes or no to a possible promotion that might change your whole life. You say yes when you join a church and become a part of a specific community of faith. You say yes or no to a marriage prospect. Perhaps you've been regretting some of the no's you said before you eventually said yes. I heard about a wealthy bachelor who died and left all of his money to three women to whom, he said, he owed all his earthly happiness. It seemed all three had said no to his proposals of marriage.

If you're a parent you find yourself saying yes or no at all sorts of crucial times in the lives of your children. In the famous biblical story of the Prodigal Son and his father, think of the courage of the father. When the son asked for his inheritance in order to leave home and go out and explore life, the father said yes. That was surely one of the high-risk adventures of all time. For parents especially, so much seems to hang on when to say no and when to say yes. Even presidents have this problem. William Howard Taft's young son was once overheard being rude to his father. "Are you going to rebuke him?" someone asked. "Well, I thought about it," was the reply. "Now, if he was speaking to me as his father, he deserves a serious rebuke, but if he was speaking to me as President, then he stands on his constitutional rights."

When to say yes and when to say no. All of life depends on these decisions. If we can't say a clear yes or a clear no, we are in trouble. We're like the man whose psychiatrist asked him after many sessions, "Don't you think you have a problem with decision making?" "Well, yes and no," was the answer. When we say both yes and no, we are in big trouble. I'm told that industry tries to hire executives who can make decisions clearly and quickly. "Yes, we'll build this; no, we'll scrap that program." If they're right 50 percent of the time, that is good enough. They're looking for people who have the courage to say yes or no. They don't always have to be right.

But faith is also a yes-or-no decision. In the biblical understanding, *faith* is a verb, not a noun. Faith is something we do. It is not something we have. We can't go out and get faith. Most of us already have a bucketful of faith. We live by faith. We have faith that other cars will stay on their own side of the road. We have faith that the water in our tap is not poisoned. Faith is something we already have. The point is what are we doing with it? I believe this is the biblical understanding of faith. Faith is not saying, "True," to a concept. When God spoke to Abraham, He asked him to do something—to leave the familiar and go into a new land. He asked Abraham to begin a pilgrimage that would take an undetermined number of years. Abraham replied by acting. He did not say, "Oh, I see. What an amazing concept. The theology of discipleship. I must write about that sometime." He had the choice of saying yes or no to God. He said yes and he went.

Moses, as well, was not asked to say, "True," to a concept but yes to a plan of action. When God met Moses at the Burning Bush, He asked him to do something. "Will you go down to Egypt and lead my people out? I want them liberated." Moses could have said, "Ah, the theology of liberation. What a revolutionary concept. I've never read anything on that subject." At first he said no, which is legitimate. But ultimately he said yes and he went.

And then there is the incredible story of Mary, that brave girl who met an angel at the well in Nazareth. The angel might have said, "Mary, good news and bad news. The good news is that the Messiah is coming. The bad news is that God thought He ought to be born of a virgin, and you've been chosen if you will say yes." Mary was not asked to accept the theology of incarnation. She had a choice of saying yes or no. She said yes; she was willing to enter into this experiment with God.

Jesus met some fishermen by the sea and asked them, "Will you follow me?" What might they have said? "Well, you see, we've got some theological problems. We heard some strange rumors about your birth. We really can't buy that story that your mother was a virgin." But Jesus was not asking them to accept difficult concepts. His question was simply, "Will you follow me?" He would deal later with their theological problems. Just then they did not need to understand all things—who He was, how He got there. A simple, clear yes was all that was required. I think there is a key here to finding spiritual wisdom. So often we preachers have tried to teach doctrine assuming that when you understood enough doctrine, you would say yes. I think we have it backward. When you say yes, spiritual wisdom follows by some mysterious work of the Holy Spirit.

In our understanding of God, you and I have a choice. Is God a concept or is He a person? If God the Creator, the inventor of you and me, is a person, then you cannot respond by saying, "I believe." Suppose someone has said to you, "I love you. You are the most wonderful person I've ever met. I want to live my life with you. Will you marry me?" You can't answer by saying, "True." That's not relevant. If someone says, "I love you. I have offered to give you my life, will you give me your life?" You can't respond with a, "True," or, "False." If we're talking about theological concepts or mathematical equations or philosophy or forms of government, we have true-or-false options. We can say, "I believe," or, "I don't believe." But the very word *believe* in the Greek means "to commit to something." For the Christian, to believe is to fling your life after a person.

A man came to see me recently about some problems. In the course of our conversation I asked him, "Are you a Christian?" "Well," he said, "Gosh, I sure try to be. I've had some great days and some bad days. I've been very faithful to God at times in my life. Right now I'm not sure." I said, "Are you married?" "Oh, yes," he said. "How can you be so sure you're married? Are you a great husband?" I asked. "Are you always there when needed, always generous, always kind, sensitive, loving—all these things—in your marriage?" "Oh," he said. "No." "But how do you know you're married?" He said, "Well, because I stood up and said before witnesses, 'Yes, I take this woman.' " I said, "You can do that with Jesus, and you can do it right now if you want to." He wanted to and he did. And I've had a number of people in my office in the short time I've been back in the pastorate who have been believers all their life but who had accepted Christian concepts and beliefs rather than saying yes to a person.

That was true of me. I grew up attending a Presbyterian church, one of the great churches in Chicago. I can't remember a time that I did not believe that Jesus was the Son of God, the Saviour who died for the sins of the world and my sins. But my life was changed in Stuttgart, Germany, during World War II, when I kneeled all by myself in a bombed-out building and said, "Jesus, if you really are the person I've always believed in, I give You my life right now. I cannot promise that I will be good or faithful. I want to be. I don't want to be who I am, but I can't promise that I will change. I hope that You will change me."

Faith is a matter of choice. In the Old Testament, we read that Joshua gave the people this choice. "I have given you a land for which ye did not labour.... choose you this day whom ye will serve..." (Joshua 24;13,15 KJV). That same choice is ours today. Most of us worship in churches we didn't build, we live in a land that has come to us through faithful people of past generations. But our choice now is whom we will serve. We can serve the gods of money, wealth, power, or religion, or we can serve the Living God.

This is the choice that Jesus gives you right now. The challenge is not complicated. It is a simple thing to say yes in a marriage ceremony. You stand up before witnesses and commit yourself to someone else for the rest of your life. But the consequences are enormous. Saying yes to a marriage partner or to God means a lifetime of faithfulness, which isn't easy. But the initial yes is very simple. You never have to wonder if you're married or if you're a Christian. You can say no, or you can say nothing—which is no. The real test is who is running your life? It's not whether or not you have good days or bad days, days of great faith or days of doubt and despair. On the best days or the worst days, who do you say is in charge of your life?

For many years I worked in New York City and counseled at my office any number of people who were wrestling with this yes-or-no decision. Often I would suggest they walk with me from my office down to the RCA Building on Fifth Avenue. In the entrance of that building is a gigantic statue of Atlas, a beautifully proportioned man who, with all his muscles straining, is holding the world upon his shoulders. There he is, the most powerfully built man in the world, and he can barely stand up under this burden. "Now that's one way to live," I would point out to my companion, "trying to carry the world on your shoulders. But now come across the street with me." On the other side of Fifth Avenue is Saint Patrick's Cathedral, and there behind the high altar is a little shrine of the boy Jesus, perhaps eight or nine years old, and with no effort He is holding the world in one hand. My point was illustrated graphically. We have a choice. We can carry the world on our shoulders or we can say, "I give up, Lord, here's my life. I give You my world, the whole world."

Perhaps you have loved Jesus all your life, but have you said yes? You're probably going to have theological problems the rest of your life. I hope you're smart enough to have theological problems. That means you're thinking about faith. In Jesus Christ, God says to us, "I have bet Myself on you, each one of you. I'm committed to you. I belong to you now. Will you follow Me? Will you say yes?"

2

The Need to Belong

I heard of a mother who returned home to find her two older sons, incidentally both Boy Scouts, beating up their little brother. Asked to explain, they said, "Well, you see, he fell in the wading pool and we are trying to give him mouth-to-mouth resuscitation. The trouble is he keeps getting up and walking away."

The story reminded me again of how often the church has tried to minister the unnecessary to the unwilling. We try to make people religious, and I believe that's the furthest thing from God's mind. If we believe in a God who can meet all of our needs, then the Church of Jesus Christ ought to be the most relevant institution in all of society. He is the ultimate relevant being, and that's the point we need to get across to those who don't know Him yet.

If the church is to be relevant, we must talk to people

about their deepest problems. In a 1978 poll 52,000 Americans were asked to name their most deadly fear. Way out in front was the answer loneliness. Most of those who responded were trying to deal with or overcome loneliness.

Dr. James Lynch of Johns Hopkins Hospital has come up with the statistics to show that loneliness is the number-one physical killer in our time. He is an exacting medical researcher whose charts and graphs indicate that discernibly lonely people are most prone to illness and death.

Thomas Wolfe, the great novelist of forty years ago, said at the end of his life, "The whole conviction of my life now rests upon the belief that loneliness, far from being a rare and curious phenomenon, is the central and inevitable fact of human existence." So the evidence that comes in from novelists, medical researchers, and public opinion polls indicates that our number-one problem is loneliness.

What do we do about loneliness? If it really is our number-one problem, then each of us must surely be an expert in loneliness. Each of us could write a Ph.D. dissertation on the shape of loneliness in our own life. If someone asked us, "What is loneliness?" we could compile a long list of answers from our own experience. Let's bear in mind that loneliness is not the same as aloneness. We can be alone and yet feel surrounded and supported by the people we have chosen to make a part of our life—sometimes even those who are no longer living. Or, we can be in the middle of a great crowd and be very lonely. Loneliness means being separated and cut off. It means being insular, having ingrown eyeballs to the point where we have no conscious connection with anybody else.

What do I know about loneliness? I recently compiled a list of what it means to be lonely, drawing from the events of my own life and the lives of my family or very intimate friends. Here are some of my personal descriptions of loneliness.

Loneliness is being single and aching physically and emotionally to share your life and your love with somebody else.

Loneliness is being married to the person of your choice, with whom you are still in love, and looking over at that spouse asleep in bed beside you and realizing that there are still large chunks of your life where loneliness reigns.

Loneliness is saying, "I love you," too late. The person who should have heard it is now dead, and all you can do is reach out and touch the corpse and say, "I hope you knew, because I never could tell you before how much you meant to me."

Loneliness is having hurt your best friend, with no way to make it right.

Loneliness is starting an organization, inviting in your best friends, and having them vote you out.

Loneliness is being told that you have a serious illness and being unable to talk about it with anyone.

Loneliness is coming to the end of your life, having used up most of the options that God has given you, and being unhappy about what you did with them. You've traded your options for a whole lot of things that turned out to be worthless. It's like winning a supermarket sweepstake—you run through the supermarket and come out with a basket heaped full of nothing but franks and beans.

Loneliness is being in the middle of a warm, friendly church and feeling that there is nobody there who really knows who you are.

Loneliness is having a secret sin so bad that you think nobody would like you if they knew.

Loneliness is having had religious parents who could only criticize, who could never affirm or hug or tell you, you were neat.

Loneliness is not living up to other people's expectations (whatever that means).

Loneliness is being a sincere believer for a long time and coming to a place where you wonder ... *Have I blown it? Did I take a wrong turn back there somewhere? Am I really in the will of God?*

Loneliness is being a coward in a crisis—when your vote or voice could have changed the decision of a committee or a group. The hour has passed, the moment is lost. You didn't speak and you're stuck with your cowardice.

All of us can make up a list of the times that we have experienced loneliness and allowed ourselves to be cut off from humanity, even from God, or so we think. I happen to believe in the devil, an evil force, the father of lies. He's a very close companion and I speak about him often. I believe that somehow he takes this inevitable fact of human existence—our loneliness—and turns it into a destructive force. Our culture is often the devil's best servant, and our culture has given us false expectations about life and what it ought to be. Our culture suggests there are four very basic ways of dealing with our loneliness.

First of all, we teach our children at a very young age that marriage is the answer to loneliness. Early on we hear as a child, and perhaps pass on to our own children, the story of the lonely girl with a mean stepmother and two ugly stepsisters. She has the blues and with good reason. Her clothes are grungy; she never goes to parties. When the rest of the family is out dancing, she's home cleaning the bathrooms. Poor old Cinderella is lonely, lonely. But one day a guy pulls up in a white Camaro with a glass shoe that just happens to fit her. They get married and what happens? They live happily ever after. So every child gets the message. Things may be tough just now but someday they'll meet Mr. or Miss Right. They will marry and they will no longer have the "lonelies." When marriage doesn't meet these expectations, most of us feel cheated. "Good grief!" we say. "I must have picked a lemon in God's grab bag of life. It's not supposed to be like this."

But of course it is. God loves us so much that He has put a longing inside of us for ultimate love, and no human relationship or circumstance will satisfy that. So the best and most fulfilling marriage, as good as it is, does not solve our basic loneliness. But we have given young people expectations of some problem-free state, and when that is not their experience, anger and frustration grow. All those happily married couples, especially the ones you meet in church, seem to have it made. They are always smiling. After the Couples' Club Potluck, we walk to the parking lot thinking, "How come I got stuck with him (or her)? All of my friends have it made."

Or, we are told that sex is the answer to our loneliness. That's what I resent most about so many of these slickly done contemporary magazines. We hear a lot of clucking about the nudity they feature, but that's not the most destructive aspect of these magazines. They are aiming at the lonely guy or gal out there and they are saying, "Hey, are you lonely? You don't have to be. Listen, if you have enough sex with enough people you won't have that problem." It is the biggest lie ever perpetrated on young people. The loneliest people in the world are hanging out in singles' bars and other places where casual sex is the deal. The Playboy philosophy, which promises intimacy and belonging, produces the very opposite. It produces alienation and self-hate.

Our culture also seems to promise that success is an answer to our loneliness: Be a success and you'll never be lonely again. If we can just get to the top in our profession—our business—we will be at the hub of a busy life, with people standing in line to be our friends. Yet you and I know that some of those people who have finally become chairman of the board are the most lonely of all—terrified at being at the top of the pyramid, of having someone discover how little they know. I think people at the top are even lonelier than the rest of us. Because they hold such power over the lives of others, they never can be sure that they are loved and appreciated for themselves. Famous rock stars seem to be tragic examples of the fact that loneliness grows in direct proportion to success.

Then there are those who believe the church is the answer to our loneliness: If you become a Christian, if you really accept Jesus, if you are really filled with the Spirit, you'll never be lonely again. Unfortunately, that isn't true either. Certainly the church is in the business of offering intimacy and community, but that doesn't mean we will have all our problems solved. In every denomination just now, clergy divorces are more and more common. We are pressed to explain this in the light of the victorious life some have been promising believers. And the guilt laid on those who continue to have problems, especially in marriage, is enormous.

There is a story about an old Scandinavian couple, Sven and Hulda, who were both born-again Pentecostal Christians. He taught Sunday school, and she sang in the choir. They had a family altar and family prayers. They went to church twice on Sundays and attended the mid-week service. But they couldn't get along. They fought all the time. They felt very guilty about their stormy relationship and they prayed about it often. One morning after their quiet time of listening to God and praying, Hulda said, "Sven, I think I've got the answer to this hopeless problem we have. I think we should pray for the Lord to take one of us to be home with Him . . . Then I can go and live with my sister."

But even those who have fulfilling marriages and who are

a part of a church full of genuine caring and community are going to experience loneliness some of the time. And I think that's part of God's plan. I really believe that loneliness is a gift of God. It is not something to be ashamed of or avoided. It's one of the best gifts God has given us. You and I were meant for belonging, intimacy, and community. We are to be an essential part of the Body of Christ, without whom the rest of the body cannot function . . . at least not as well. You and I were made to belong to God—that is the ultimate relationship—and then to a cluster of His people. The one thing that drives us to seek that state is our loneliness.

Loneliness is a gift not unlike pain. God wills for you and me to be well physically until we die. That's His best plan. Sickness is not part of His best plan. If we eat the wrong things or eat too much, we experience pain. If we step on a broken bottle at the beach, we feel pain. Pain gives us a message. It says stop eating or take care of that bleeding foot. Pain prevents us from continuing as though nothing had happened. We've got to stop and take care of whatever hurts so that we can continue to live. Were it not for the pain, we would just keep on going and die. So as pain forces us to find healing, loneliness drives us to love and community and God.

There's no way to escape loneliness. The key is to use it constructively. Our Lord was totally human, without sin but totally human. And being totally human, He was exactly like us in every way. As the ultimate Person He had ultimate loneliness. The New Testament tells us what He did with His loneliness. We read the account of His night of prayer in

Gethsemane just before He was betrayed and arrested. He is at the very end of His earthly life, and He is saying two things in that final prayer (*see* Mark 14). He is feeling, first of all, cut off from God, not sure if He is really in God's will. To put it in today's language, He is saying, "Father, maybe I blew it. Maybe there was a fork in the road I missed, and now I'm headed for this valley of pain and humiliation and annihilation. Perhaps that wasn't what You planned for me. But even if it is Your will, Father, I'm not sure I can go through with it. It's too costly." It was a time of ultimate loneliness, and being totally human, Jesus couldn't escape it. But He had two options. He could either hide His loneliness and go off and pray alone or He could share it. He asked three of His disciples, Peter, James, and John, to join Him in His lonely vigil. He was able to say, "I'm lonely, I'm frightened. Will you three come and keep me company in this last few hours of my life?" They went, even though they kept falling asleep, and because of their account of that agonizing night, Jesus shared His loneliness with all of us.

Hazel and I have taken a number of groups to the Holy Land in past years. As a kind of spiritual "voyeur," I'm always intrigued by what particular place, among those many holy places, turns people on. Gethsemane is certainly one of those places. *Gethsemane,* in Hebrew, simply means "olive press." There was an olive grove on the side of the hill, and there was an olive press in that grove. Jesus and the three disciples went out to an orchard that looked across the Kidron Valley to Jerusalem. There are still olive trees on that hillside—two of them at least 2,000 years old. They have un-

covered the remains of an old olive press. So it's almost certainly the garden where our Lord knelt and prayed that
night. We pilgrims who visit there today are always moved,
overwhelmed by the cost of God's love for us. We stand
with tears flowing as we think of what happened—probably
at that very spot. It is the place where Jesus let us know the
depth of His suffering and the cost of His love for us. He
shared His utter loneliness.

And Jesus says to us, "And this is My commandment,
love one another as I have loved you" (*see* John 13:34). He
has shown us how to deal with our loneliness. We can't escape it. But if we share it with someone else, God gives us
the gift of community, of intimacy, and of love.

Some years ago I went to a meeting where Dr. Bob Pierce,
founder of World Vision, was speaking. He was a worldwide
evangelist and missionary, then near the end of his life. He
had spent his life founding orphanages in Korea, rescuing
children from death and starvation. As an evangelist he
converted thousands of people all over the world. He was
speaking to a small group, and most of us were in awe of
what God had accomplished through this one committed
man. But his message took us by surprise. He told us about
an incident that had occurred one Christmas Eve when he
was in Stockholm traveling with the Korean Children's
Choir. He made a call home and talked to all the members
of his family, wishing them a Merry Christmas. Finally, the
littlest one got the phone. "Oh, Daddy," she said. "I wish I
was an orphan so I could be with you on Christmas Eve."
He told us, "My heart broke. And I say to you now that I'm

not sure if I *was* in the will of the Lord all those years. I know God has used me—God uses whatever you give Him. But I'm still wondering if perhaps I did not have a prior commitment to my own family, my own children? Was it God's will for me to be away so much? I simply don't know." Somehow as he opened his heart to us and showed us the pain and uncertainty he had experienced, the Spirit of the Living Christ filled that room. As Bob Pierce shared his loneliness and confusion, we felt loved.

Do you want to live at this level? Suppose some Saturday night your pastor calls you to come over to the parsonage perhaps with two or three others. When you arrive he might say, "Come in, I hope you can spare the whole evening. I've got the coffeepot on. It's been a bad week for me. I really haven't prayed sincerely all week and haven't talked civilly to my wife for ten days. I'm mad at God. I hate myself. Tomorrow is Sunday. I'm supposed to preach and bring the Good News to God's people and I'm in no shape to do it. And so tonight I'm going to wrestle with God and see if He can find me again, put me in my right mind, and fill me one more time with the Spirit. I'm not sure that He can and I'm not sure that I'll let Him. I know He wants to, but it's one of those dark nights of the soul. Would you three friends simply keep me company? I'm terrified." Could you handle that kind of situation—accept that kind of pastor, one who doesn't always have it together? That's what the gift of loneliness is all about.

Just about a month before I came to Seattle from Florida, I had a call from a friend in a distant city. He is a lay evangelist and head of a big business. I hadn't seen him in several years. He called to get some advice on something, but somehow we never really connected. We had a nice Christian conversation. Did you ever have one of those? We were both very nice and very polite but just a little testy. After I hung up, I felt rotten. An hour later the phone rang again and it was the same friend. "Bruce," he said, "I can't go back to work. I'm really upset about our phone conversation. Let's start again. Let me tell you what's been happening to me over these last years. They have been the worst years of my life. Everything has turned sour—my business, my family, my kids, even my Christian work. The last six weeks have been unbearable. I'm really in bad shape." I told him how grateful I was he had called and began to share some of the pain and isolation I had gone through in recent years. We were two little hurting boys talking long distance about who we really were and love came in, all because my friend shared with me the gift of his loneliness.

As you deal with your loneliness, I would urge you to remember three things: First, your loneliness is inevitable. You can't escape it. Accept it. Second, see it as God's gift to you. Were it not for loneliness, you and I would never reach out for God or for each other. New relationships are scary, but loneliness drives us to seek them. Finally, as you reach out to share the gift of loneliness with others, expect God to be there even as He was at Gethsemane. Christian community is loneliness shared with God and one another.

3

Time to Come Home

A man I know went to his class reunion a few months ago. I asked him how it went. "It was terrible," he confessed. "My classmates were all so old and fat and bald that none of them recognized me." Sometimes revisiting past scenes is not altogether happy. At best, there is a poignancy in seeing the familiar people and places where we were once so at home.

But I would like you to remember with me right now the first time you were homesick. Can you remember where you were . . . how old you were . . . the home you were separated from . . . the family members you left? I remember vividly the first time I felt estranged and separated from the place where I belonged. I was seven years old. My parents had lovingly sent me to a church camp. I went off to Camp Gray on the shores of Lake Michigan for two weeks. And for two weeks I was sick to my stomach. The nights were interminable, and I remember lying in my bunk, wondering how I could go home and still save face. If only I could go home. I didn't belong with all those strange people. My only positive memory was that I had my first fight at that camp and won. With great joy I remember beating up the son of a McCormick Seminary professor. But the feeling I remember most is one of homesickness. "Would I ever be home again?"

I'm sure you can remember times like that. When you're homesick it is more than missing a place. Usually we are missing someone who cares for us and is waiting for our return. And if that person or persons is somewhere else, why are we here? Will the time ever come when we can go home again? Somehow that still-popular song "Tie a Yellow Ribbon" captures those feelings again for us. The character in the song is wandering in the far country like the Prodigal Son. He has blown it, done dumb things, things for which he is ashamed. Finally he writes a letter saying, "Hey, family, I'd like to come home. If you don't want me back, I can't blame you. But if you do, would you put a yellow ribbon on the old tree out in the yard? I'll ride by and if I don't see a ribbon, I'll just keep moving on. If I see a yellow ribbon, I'll come home." Most of us still get choked up when we get to the place where our hero goes by and finds the tree so full of yellow ribbons he can't see the branches. It may be a little corny, but most of us were so gripped by the idea, that the yellow ribbon became a national symbol when our American hostages were being held in Iran.

This is what homecoming is all about. No matter where

we've been or what we've done, there's a time to come
home. We belong. This is the message at the heart of the
Gospel. The Good News in Jesus is that there is a homecoming, a gathering for all of us. He has come to make it
OK for you and me to come home to the place where we
really belong. We don't belong in a far country. We're not at
home with some of the foolish things we've done. And who
is God really? He is the center of the gathering. He is your
real Father, who figuratively ties a million yellow ribbons in
the tree and says, "I know. I understand. Yes, you've been
dumb. Yes, you've been selfish. Yes, you've been foolish.
But come home." Is that news too good to be true? It is
really the heart of what you and I believe as Christians.

Perhaps the most poignant story Jesus ever told was the
parable of the father with two sons. Those of us who are parents have only to hear the opening line—that a certain man
had two sons—and we immediately react, "Oh, Oh, trouble." If you've had two or more children, you are impressed
by the miracle of personality. Each child is entirely unique.
In the story Jesus tells, one son says to the father, "I want to
go out in the world and make my fortune." Now most of us
parents know our children pretty well. The father probably
knew exactly, or within certain limits, what his son was capable of. The story is incredible because (and just think of
this if you pride yourself on being a godly parent) the father
does not just say, "It's OK. You can go." Knowing his child
well enough to predict the disaster that will result, the father
nevertheless says (to put it in today's vernacular), "Here's a
whole fistful of traveler's checks." He pays the bill for this

foolhardy adventure. Love does not control or manipulate. You and I as parents cannot always control the children we love, even for their own good. Wanting the best for our children, we try to protect them from foolish decisions. But God doesn't do that. God says, "If you must go, here's a fistful of traveler's checks. I'll miss you." You can bet there are tears. But the father Jesus describes says you're free to come and you're free to go.

This parable teaches us a second thing about the nature of God's love—God is not a rescuer. The father does not send a CARE package to the far country. And you better believe people then were just like people today. Those who journeyed to the far country, as traveling salesmen, or off on a theater tour, or whatever, were eager to come back with the bad news. "Oh, let me tell you about your son. You won't believe what he's doing." Those stories must have broken the father's heart, but he doesn't write, he doesn't send food or money. The son knows the way home, and the father gives the son the dignity of managing his own life. The son could live there as long as he wanted and though the father is brokenhearted, there are no attempts to rescue the boy.

A few months before we left Sanibel, Florida, and moved to Seattle, we were involved with a wonderful Christian family who had an adopted son who had gone to the far country and lived it up in every way—sex, drugs, booze, whatever. They did everything to help him. They went to see him, sent money, shamed him, prayed for him. They finally came to the place where they said, "We can't do anymore." And they quit. We just heard about a month ago that their son came home. Not because somebody tried to bring him home but because he got homesick. He came home healed and the rejoicing is enormous.

The turning point in the parable Jesus told is when the son in the far country comes to himself. Just what does that mean? I heard about an old country parson who preached on that subject. He said, "This man was so poor he sold his coat to buy bread, then he sold his shirt to buy bread. Finally, he sold his underwear for bread and then he came to himself." We'd like to call that experience of "coming to himself" a conviction of sin. But there's no indication that this young man is convicted of anything. He does not say, "I've done a terrible thing." What he says is, "How dumb I am to be here starving. My father's hired servants live better than this. I can't go back and be a son but since my father is a compassionate man, maybe I can go back and live as one of his servants. I will go home and I will say to him (because this may make points with the old man), 'Father, I've sinned.'" But his motivation is to better himself. He comes to himself when he assesses his situation. What am I doing here? I don't belong here. I'm out of place. I'm going back where things are better.

Is it possible that you and I can really begin again? I recently heard a pertinent story about George Bernard Shaw, the famous playwright and critic. At age ninety he was very ill and close to death. He was so weak he could speak only with great effort. But at one point he leaned over and said to his nurse, "Dear, would you do me a favor? When the doctor comes in and says that I'm dead, would you ask for a second opinion?" Usually we need a second opinion on our condition, whatever it is. If somebody has said you're dead (or hopeless, which is about the same thing), get a second opinion from God. If you've been told, "You've had it; you've blown it," God wants to give you a second opinion. You can come home again.

I spent a day recently visiting one of the great rescue missions in our town. I toured the building and met many of the men. The director was taking me around, and I was moved to see the compassion that those people have in caring for the lost and the least. Toward the end of my visit, the director made an interesting observation. "You know it's a strange thing. When I ask the older men and women who come here about their problems, they invariably say, 'I'm a failure, that's why I'm here. I've been dumb and foolish and wasted my life.' They have a clear sense of right and wrong, good and evil, and they're ready to deal with their failures. The younger people who come in, those in their teens and twenties, have no sense of right and wrong. They have no insight into the cause of their problems. They tend to blame circumstances, society, their parents. There's no sense of having done anything wrong."

But I think the implication of Jesus' parable is that you don't necessarily have to have a conviction of sin to come home. You can come home when you realize that you don't need to continue living in this foolish way. There's something better for us. God has something better. Perhaps it's easier to come home if you are doing destructive things and want to change. But how hard it is if you're living a life of responsibility and respectability to confess that you're lonely and you long to come home.

When I lived in Florida, I had a retired neighbor who was remarkably active. He served on the City Council; he was a senior vestryman in his church. One weekend he went off to a gathering led by lay people where he made a new beginning with God. Later, he was sharing this experience with me and another neighbor, an avowed atheist. I said, "Dick, what really happened?" "It's hard to describe," he said. "I'll tell you I found that I'm loved and that Jesus is real. It was the most exciting weekend of my life." The conversation really puzzled my nonchurched neighbor, and he spoke to me about it later. "Bruce, I really don't understand what happened to Dick. He has always been a good man." I agreed, "Yes, he has. And it must be much harder for a good man to come home than a bad one."

Finally, this story of the father and the Prodigal Son teaches us that love does not make conditions. Love does not say, "Well, OK, you're back home now. You must never leave again." A cartoon I saw years ago in *The New Yorker* caught the astonishing dimensions of the unconditional love God has for us. The drawing was a biblical scene of the Prodigal Son, the father, the neighbors, all in their white robes. The father is about to carve a huge roasted calf when he turns to his son with a worried look and says, "Now, after all son, this is the fourth fatted calf."

Can you really believe that the Father will kill four or forty-four fatted calves for you? Do you really believe that you can come home again and again? Each time you leave, you break His heart, you hurt yourself, and you hurt others. But there is a family gathering where you can come home again and again. The truly tragic figure is the son who stayed home and never did an irresponsible thing. He couldn't rejoice and join the party. He was furious. He says, "I don't understand. I've been here all the time and you never gave me a goat for a party with my friends." Someone suggested that with his niggardly spirit one mutton chop would be enough to serve the whole group.

You see, it's not enough to be in the household of God doing the right thing. When we insist that we have never done anything wrong, we can't come home. In the parable, the father says, "Son, don't you understand? Everything I have is yours." But the son wanted his wages. He wanted exactly what his brother got. The father tried to explain, "No, no, son, it's all yours. Take everything I've got." But the elder brother insisted, "I just want what's coming to me." He was as lost as his brother had been. In insisting on what was due him, he missed out on the riches the father wanted to give him.

Jesus came to tell us that it's time to come home, whoever we are. That's what the Good News is all about. Come as you are!

4

Who Are You?

On a recent visit to Seattle our oldest son, who is a newspaper reporter, brought me the current copy of a large "underground" newspaper. He called my attention to the section called, "Personals." I want to share some of those "personals" with you now, just as my son did with me. I do so without making any moral judgments, though that would not be difficult. There is a far more serious issue at stake than morals or ethics.

> Unhappily married fun-loving professional man in 40's sks. single woman for fun, dining and romancing.

> Single white male seeks close relationship but not marriage with tall attractive wf, vegetarian preferred.

Single white male 5'5" looking for small woman. Interests are music, movies, golf and backgammon. Send picture.

Soon to be paroled male looking for serious single female to correspond with. In 20's and aiming for self-improvement.

College professor and Marxist sympathizer looking for female who wants to help change the world. Must love cats.

White female who is tired of dieting is looking for male in his 40s interested in a growth opportunity. Interests TV and eating.

Sophisticated 33-year-old male, educated in Europe, seeks gorgeous brown-eyed blonde with a great shape for disco and other fun and games. Send photo.

Serious-minded male in 50's wants to meet like-minded female—no smoking, drugs, or divorce. Must like classical music and museums.

Honest Christian Gentleman mid 50's seeking serious, faithful lady in her 40's for marriage. If honest and faithful, please reply.

When my son Peter read these to me he said, "Do you know, Dad, we could simplify all this if we had a Dewey decimal system for rating people. It would save so much time to say a 348.36 wants to meet a 517.93."

Well, I think Peter fully understood the frightening implications of these "personals." These people, with either honorable or dishonorable intentions, are trying to meet a member of the opposite sex by putting themselves on the market as a commodity looking for another commodity. They are presenting themselves as a package made up of age, sex, habits, and interests. They have lost their sense of personhood.

There is a battle going on between God and the enemy for our very souls. The classical writers of the past understood this clearly. In *Faust* we find a man who bargains with the devil. The devil wants to possess his soul, and he makes the offer attractive enough to close the deal. And exactly what is your soul? Your soul is who you are, your very essence, your identity, that which God had in mind before you were born. If you give that up, you have lost everything. We read in the New Testament, "What shall it profit a man, if he shall gain the whole world, and lose his own soul?" (Mark 8:36 KJV).

I am convinced that this ancient battle between God and our ultimate enemy still continues with us today. We may laugh at the devil, but his strategy is more powerful than ever. Albert Camus, one of our great existential writers and novelists, said, "Man is the only creature who refuses to be what he is." Zebras and monkeys, polar bears and butterflies have no identity problems. Only we humans have the capacity to deny who we are or to try to be something else.

I have a good friend who is a psychiatrist in the Black Forest area of Germany. Walther Lechler is a Christian and, I think, one of the most exciting and eclectic psychiatrists in all Europe. His clinic at Bad Herenalb is for alcoholics and general neurotics, people not unlike you and me. The bro-

chure describing his clinic says, among other things, "Come
here to discover that you are not the dwarf of your fears nor
the giant of your dreams. Come and find out who you really
are." You see, that is the most primal and basic search you
and I are engaged in.

The personals in the underground paper point up the fact
that there is a powerful force at work in our culture to rob us
of our identity. This cultural force says that you are not a
person, but a commodity. You are a thing. You are a package. You are a number. Look in your wallet and see how
you are identified by the government or by your bank. You
have a social security number and credit card. You are a
number to the phone company and a five-digit zip code to
your postman.

A recent movie suggested that we rate members of the
opposite sex by numbers on a scale of one to ten. This is
merely an extension of the idea communicated in the newspaper "personals." A newly divorced friend was telling me
recently how totally unfulfilling the marriage had been for
both him and his wife. I asked, "Just why did you marry this
girl?" "Because she was a fifteen!" was his answer. I believe
there is something insidious about categorizing another
human being as a three, a seven, a ten, or a fifteen. We have
reduced people to commodities.

For centuries Christians have been trying to understand
the term "the mark of the beast" in the Bible. Certainly one
explanation is that there is an evil force who wants to replace your identity with a number and to make you a commodity. One of the central themes of the Bible is that when

we encounter God, we discover that He wants to give us a name—our true name.

One of the Bible's many examples of this kind of encounter is the account of Jacob wrestling with an angel by the brook Jabbok. The first time I saw this lonely valley between low hills where a little brook still meanders, I was deeply moved. In my mind's eye I could imagine the struggle that took place three thousand years ago when someone not unlike one of us was facing the crisis of his life. His past had caught up with him. He had cheated his brother, deceived his father, and tricked his father-in-law. The consequences were now crashing down upon him, and it was the dark night of the soul for Jacob as he wrestled with God all night by this hauntingly lonely and lovely brook. His opponent had crippled him, but Jacob persevered. Just before dawn he said, "I will not let you go unless you bless me." At that point, the angel said to him, "Who are you?" And the answer was, "Jacob."

Now Jacob is the name that his parents gave him. Remember that he and his brother, Esau, were twins. He was the second to come out of the womb and was born trying to grab his brother's heel. In Jewish custom the firstborn gets everything and the second born gets nothing. This little infant arrived in this world struggling to supplant his brother. A power struggle began very early on, as it does in your family and mine. And those witnessing that unusual birth said, "Look at little Cheat (or sneak, for that's what Jacob means)." In all the ensuing years that was his name—little Cheat. But little Cheat became big Cheat. His family named him something destructive because they thought it was cute, and it shaped Jacob's life.

What has your family named you? How do you appear in their eyes? Do they say, "Here comes that mess; here comes the clumsy one? Here comes our problem child? Here comes the rule-breaker?" Or do they say, "Here comes our darling—the precious one who can't ever do anything wrong?" Somewhere along the line the family name sticks, and you become that which your parents have called you.

I heard about a minister's son who spent the whole night carousing and arrived home at 5 A.M. smelling of strong drink. His father greeted him the next morning at breakfast with, "Good morning, Son of Satan." "Good morning, Father," was the cheerful answer. Unfortunately, most of us don't have the capacity to slough off the names our parents have given us as easily as that young man. Most of us tend to become what we are called.

Or, perhaps, even though your parents haven't given you a name with a negative connotation, they have nevertheless communicated somehow that you are of less worth than you really are. Brooks Adams, son of Charles Francis Adams, one of our former ambassadors to Great Britain, tells a moving story about his boyhood. Once his father took him fishing for a whole day. Brooks recorded that day in his diary, "Spent the day fishing with my father; it was the most glorious day of my life." He had had his father's attention for a whole day. And ever after, he kept referring back to that day as one that had changed his life. Years later, upon his father's death, he found among his possessions a diary for that same period. He looked up the entry for that memorable day and found that his father had written, "Spent the day fishing with my son; a wasted day." His father may have loved him dearly, but he nevertheless felt a day spent with him was a wasted day. If you are unimportant to your parents, they have labeled you and given you a negative identity.

Even Jesus was labeled. We read in our New Testament about Philip's attempt to convince his friend Nathanael that he had found the Messiah. When Nathanael learns that it is Jesus of Nazareth, he says, "A Nazarene? Can any good thing come out of Nazareth?" (*see* John: 45,46). He was one of those people who labeled others by where they were from. Society still does that. Oh, you're from Texas, or Hollywood, or Brooklyn, or Pumpkin Gulch. Right away we have projected an image of what you're like. You're already in a box because you are from the Bronx, Boston, or Peoria. We have this stereotyped kind of thinking. I think it's all part of the devil's plot to take away our individuality. In some societies (and ours is one of them) the term "senior citizen" has a negative label. The older person is no longer expected to make a contribution. But in a different society the older a person is the more he is honored and respected and listened to. What makes the difference? The label! We are labeled by all sorts of things—our incomes, our jobs, the clubs we belong to, even the church we attend.

What happens if you choose a college that stresses competitive sports? If you are an intellectual instead of a jock, you tend to see yourself as second class for the rest of your

life. An athlete at a school that prides itself on the academic
has the same experience. Unfortunately, our environment
tends to label us, for better or for worse.

In this whole matter of our identity I believe that God
wants to give us three great gifts. First He wants to give us
the gift of knowing whose we are. We belong to Him. The
precise words in the Bible are, "Ye have not chosen me, but
I have chosen you" (KJV). When we acknowledge that and
say yes to God, we know whose we are. The most important
decision any of us can ever make is to say yes to God's great
affirmation of us.

But after we have settled whose we are, God can give us
the gift of knowing who we are. When Jacob wrestled with
the angel, he was actually wrestling with God, who was asking, "Who are you?" When Jacob answered, "I'm a cheat,"
God gave him a new name, erasing the name his parents
had given him. His new name is Israel, which means prince.
And from that moment on the cheat became a prince, from
whom all believers have since been named. We Christians
are the new Israel, named for the one whose name was
changed. God gave him his right name, and he became what
God called him.

Jesus gave Nathanael a new identity, as well—the same
Nathanael who was so ready to label others by their home-
town. We don't know what Nathanael's parents had in mind
when they named him, or what that name came to mean.
"Dumb old Nathanael, playboy Nathanael." But when
Jesus Christ meets him He says, "Look here. This is a rare
specimen. An Israelite in whom there is no guile" (*see* John 1:

47–49). There aren't many of those around even now, Israelites or Presbyterians. Most of us have lots of guile. Jesus saw a man who was transparent, with no hidden motives. Nathanael must have been struck with the accuracy of this description, for he exclaimed, "How did you know me?" Jesus said, "I know you. I saw you under a fig tree before Philip called you." Nathanael's response is a declaration of faith, "You are the Son of God." God can do that for you and me as well. People around us—parents, spouse, friends—may never discern who we really are; but God does and He can give us our real name.

It's so liberating to realize we are special. I was reading recently about Harvard University observing its 300th anniversary. In the midst of this great celebration, the freshman class came marching down the street carrying a banner that said, "Harvard has been waiting 300 years for us." Instead of worrying about their worthiness to be at a school with such an awesome tradition, they believed their presence would bring about Harvard's finest hour.

That's the kind of hope God gave Jacob when He named him Prince. Jesus gave a new name to Simon as well. He believed in him, believed that he would no longer be the impetuous, vacillating person he had been. He named him Peter, the Rock. Peter became a rock. Jesus communicated to the least important woman in a Samaritan village that she was important. How? By spending time with her. By listening to her. He honored her questions and He asked about the most intimate details of her life. After that encounter, she ran through the town crying, "Listen! I have met the

Messiah, someone who knows all about me and who let me know I'm somebody. Whatever you all think of me, I've met the one who knows who I really am" (*see* John 4:1–42).

But after we find out whose we are and who we are, we discover that we are not alone. God gives us a new family. It is one of His choosing, not one that we choose. All of us who are a part of a community of Believers did not choose the other members. We are God's gift to each other. He tells us whose we are, who we are, and where we belong. We belong to each other. We are blessers one of another—giving each other new names, calling forth hidden gifts, and being ministers one to another.

I met a minister like that when I was in the infantry during World War II. He was our battalion surgeon and his name was Doc O'Rourke. Doc O'Rourke had worked his way through medical school by playing professional football. He was a great, friendly Irishman with a big smile and flashing eyes. I can remember the many times we were under fire within hundreds of yards of the Germans when a wounded man would cry out. Who responded? The chaplain and Doc O'Rourke, carrying Red Cross flags and the litter, risking their lives to rescue one wounded man.

Just once during combat I went on sick call to an aid station about two miles back from the front. It was just a basement with three walls left; the building itself had been blown away.

It was wintertime in the Vosges Mountains, bitter cold and snowing. It seemed as though there were a hundred of us lined up on sick call to see the harried battalion surgeon.

Each person was asked first of all, "Open your shirt up," for an examination with a stethoscope. But each time before putting that cold metal on someone's chest, Doc would walk over and dip it into a pot of hot water. I was deeply touched watching that simple act. To Doc O'Rourke we were human beings. We were not just pieces of meat being patched up. To Doc O'Rourke each one of us was special. We discovered our worth as we saw how he treated us. You and I have that same power to communicate to others that they are special. At home, in our schools, at work, we can let people know that they are important to God and therefore they are important to us.

Who am I? Jeremiah asked this question. He writes that the word of the Lord came to him and he wrote these words, "Before I formed you in the womb I knew you, and before you were born I consecrated you; I appointed you a prophet to the nations" (Jeremiah 1:5 RSV). That doesn't just apply to Jeremiah. God thought of you before you were born and before your parents were born, and He called you by name. He had an identity for you. He still does. Don't settle for anything less.

5

You and Your Vocation

One Sunday evening one of those things we dread most
happened. My wife and I had been invited to a supper party.
We were a little late leaving, because of a prior engagement,
and we left the house in a rush. We had the address in
mind—a house on the corner of something like Twenty-
third Street and Thirty-fifth Avenue. We got to that address,
and the house we remembered was not there. We said,
"Good grief! Maybe it's Thirty-second Street and Fifty-
third Avenue." We went to every possible combination of
those four numbers and still didn't find the familiar house.
We decided to look it up in the phone book and pulled in to
use a public telephone booth. Neither of us had our reading
glasses. We could not read the phone book. Next, we discovered we had no change anyway. Finally, we stopped at a
strange house and asked to use the phone. Eventually we

made it to our appointment. It seemed a timely prelude for the two questions I want you to consider: "Where do you want to go?" and, "How do you plan to get there?"

A minister friend in New England sent me a sermon he preached recently on the topic "Where will you be when you get where you're going?" And, of course, the whole mystery of your identity is tied up with where you're going. Where you hope to be and how you hope to get there is a big part of understanding your gifts and your uniqueness.

Most of us tend to answer the question "Who are you?" by telling what we do for a living. But you are not your job. Your job is not your vocation. Suppose you were living 2,000 years ago and had an opportunity to ask the Apostle Paul, "Who are you?" One possible answer could be, "I'm a tentmaker. I am a very efficient, competent, creative tentmaker. My bids are competitive. I have up-to-date designs. I think I am one of the best in the business. I spend forty or fifty hours a week making tents. On the side, I do a little preaching and some small-group work." This would likely be a very accurate answer. The majority of Paul's time was spent making tents—at one time with Priscilla and Aquila. Forty or fifty hours a week might have been occupied that way. But somehow I don't think that would be his answer to your question. I think he might say something like this, "Let me tell you, God has given me a calling to bring the Good News of Jesus Christ to the world. Incidentally, I make tents and I spend a good part of my day doing that."

Ananias, the man who was sent to pray with Paul in Damascus, was an ordinary layman with a steady job. Perhaps he worked in the local sandal factory. He might have been a money lender. He might even have worked in some first-century McDonald's—some kind of fast-food shish kebab chain. The point is he had a job and he was supposed to go to work on the morning the Lord spoke to him about visiting Saul. He was told something like this, "Don't go to work this morning. I've got a job for you. Phone in and say you'll be late." He argues at first. He's sure the Lord has made a mistake. But finally he obeys. Ananias knows his vocation is to serve the Lord. Incidentally, he makes his living at a job.

I love the story of the Prophet Amos. He is no professional. He arrives in the Washington, D.C., of his time and says to the king, "We are in big trouble as a nation." They ask who he is, very likely in tones that mean, "Who do you think you are, anyway?" He says, "Listen, I am not a professional prophet. I am not a seminary-trained preacher. I am not a philosopher. You want to know who I am? I'm a shepherd and a fig-picker. That's what I do for a living fifty, sixty, or eighty hours a week. But my vocation is to come here and say we are in serious trouble and to tell you what we should do about it." We have a present-day Amos in our time in Eric Hoffer, the longshoreman. He has spent most of his life unloading boats in California forty or more hours a week. But that's not who he is. He is writing books to challenge the way America lives. In his spare time he is fulfilling his vocation.

Suppose you were asked, "Who are you and what do you do?" Your vocation and your job may be two very different things. You may say, "Well here's what I do forty hours a week to make a living, to pay the rent, and buy the groceries. But my real vocation takes five hours a week. That's a time when I teach a class or do volunteer work at the hospital or whatever. This is the work I am called to do. But I have a job to make a living." If that's the case, you're in the company of Amos, of Paul, of Ananias, and a great host of biblical people who had both a job and a vocation.

Then there are those people for whom the job and the vocation are parallel. That's a special privilege it seems to me—to have a job in the area of your vocation. But it is also easier to confuse the two. And they are not quite the same. For example, teaching is a job not a vocation. Your vocation is to call forth gifts in students and motivate them to learn. Practicing law is a job; your vocation is to see that there is equal justice under the law individually and corporately. Medicine, whether you're a doctor or a nurse, is a job, but healing is a vocation.

For you mothers or fathers who stay home and care for your families, homemaking is simply a job, but growing people is your vocation. We're told that John Wesley's mother, Susanna, had eleven children and yet she spent an hour alone with each one every week talking to them about their spiritual life. She understood that running a household was a job but she had a broader vocation—to grow people. When I tell my wife that story, she always reminds me that Susanna had live-in help. Nevertheless, she had a vision of what her vocation was quite apart from her job. Mother Teresa reminds us that being a nun is a job but bringing the love of Christ to the dying and hungry people of Calcutta is a vocation. Selling is a job; helping people acquire what they need, *really need,* is a vocation. Designing or constructing buildings is a job, but improving the way people live is a vocation.

Jim Rouse, who built the city of Columbia, Maryland, was challenged to do so as part of a Christian congregation. A mortgage banker, he was building shopping centers and malls when God gave him a concern for the impersonal and destructive aspects of life in most of our American cities. He decided to build a model city that could provide an alternative. Jim found his vocation in his attempt to build a new city that would enable and promote personal relationships.

Counseling is a job. Being a friend to those who come for advice is a vocation. Politics is a job; building a just and humane society is a vocation. Would that we had more politicians with a genuine sense of vocation. Preaching is a job— my job just now—but my vocation is to enable the people of God to be everything they are meant to be.

What are you hoping to accomplish with your life? When you get where you're going, where will you be? If you spend forty years being a lawyer, engineer, salesperson, nurse, what will you have accomplished? If you've had only a job all those years, you may not have accomplished very much. If God has given you a vocation along with that job, you will have accomplished a great deal. It's the old case of the means versus the end. Some of you are students who are studying and preparing to qualify for a particular job, but your job will not necessarily be your vocation. Your job will be a platform from which you can exercise your skills in pursuit of your vocation.

I heard about a businessman who turned his successful business over to his son and made him the new president. The company made drills of all sizes and shapes. Of course, the encumbent vice-presidents were very unhappy that they were to be working for this inexperienced young man. When he called his first staff meeting to focus on long-range planning, they were not exactly cooperative. The vice-president in charge of long-range planning said, "Pardon me, sonny . . . er, sir, we have covered all this. We have done our homework. We know exactly what the market needs and wants. We are planning on everything from quarter-inch to one-inch drills, self-contained power units, hookup units, you name it, we have planned for it." The young man was patient. "This meeting is not to talk about drills," he explained. "There is no market for drills. The market is for holes. People are buying holes. People want triangular-shaped holes or square holes or round holes. Drills are simply a means to getting the kind of holes they want. Have you surveyed how we can make holes better with whatever means, drill or otherwise?" This young man did not confuse the ends with the means. Don't confuse the means of your life—your job—with the thing that you want to produce as a lasting accomplishment.

Jesus said, "I came that you might have life and have it

more abundantly" (*see* John 10:10). Each of us separately has a calling from Him. There is something He has for us to do both in terms of a job and a vocation. You never retire from your vocation. Jobs may come and go. But God can call you to your vocation, a particular way in which you are to serve Him in His world. All the exciting people I've known have had this sense of vocation. One of my oldest friends is Ralston Young, a neighbor out in New Jersey for many years. He was written up in *Reader's Digest* years ago as "The Most Unforgettable Character I Have Ever Met." He was the famous Redcap 42, whose job was to carry bags at Grand Central Station in New York. His vocation was loving the people whose bags he carried. He said, "Everybody taking a train out of Grand Central isn't going on a honeymoon. Many are going to funerals. Many are about to be separated from family and friends for a long time. Some are going to prison." He had a prayer meeting three days a week at twelve noon on Track 13 in a cold, unlighted railroad coach. All sorts of people would come—businessmen, secretaries, worn-out preachers—to the Track 13 prayer meeting with Redcap 42. He had a vocation. Carrying bags was his job.

Elisabeth Kübler-Ross, a doctor, has found her vocation in helping the dying and those who care for them to understand the dynamics of death. Maggie Kuhn, founder of the Gray Panthers, has found her vocation. She's helping people over sixty-five to discover that the best years are ahead. Bill Stringfellow, a lawyer, described by Karl Barth a decade ago as the greatest theologian in America, found the Lord when he was at Harvard. He graduated from Harvard Law School at the top of his class. Over lunch one day in New York he told me that his vocation was not law. That was simply a job. His vocation was to see that the poor had access to legal representation. Stringfellow, Harvard Law School's top graduate, went to New York City's Harlem, rented a cold-water, fifth-floor flat and opened his law practice. His vocation wasn't law; it was to serve the oppressed, the lowest and the least of the land.

My mother, who died at ninety-three, had a vocation. Until she was eighty-five she was healthy and strong and full of vim and vigor. She worked five days a week full-time doing volunteer work at Cook County Hospital, selling secondhand goods in a thrift shop in the slums, and tutoring a ghetto child with reading problems. When she quit her vocation, she began to fall apart mentally and physically. Was that a cause and effect? I think so. When she moved to a retirement village, she lost her vocation and with it something of who she was.

If you're trying to find your vocation, let me give you some guidelines:

1. *First of all, listen to God.* Let Him tell you what He is hoping you will be when you get where you are going. I believe God wants you to be accountable for a certain group of people somewhere and for their physical, mental, emotional, economic, or spiritual well-being. Where is your group? Be praying about that. Ananias knew what his vocation was—God had made it clear to him, as He did with Amos and the Apostle Paul.

2. *Claim your uniqueness*—no one has been where you've been. All the hurt, the pain, the gifts, and experiences that you have had have equipped you to see life as nobody else sees it. We have a member of our congregation writing books right now where handicapped children are the heroes and heroines—something that as far as I know has not been done as yet. She is writing out of some of the pain and the hurt and hardship of her own experience, and those books are certain to bless many. Each of us has been where no one else has been. God gives us unique eyes to see the world around us and make our particular contribution.

3. *Be open to change.* Don't believe that you must be what you have been. William James, pioneer psychologist, wrote years ago, "The ideas gained by men before they are 25 are practically the only ideas they shall have in their lives." If true, that's a tragedy. Be open to change. God may show you a whole new thing. Be open to change and to growth in terms of your vocation.

4. *Don't think in existing categories.* Don't be limited by the fact that you are not a professional, that you don't have credentials. All of society seems to be breaking loose in this area. Someone wrote recently, "Our society is becoming accustomed to the 28-year-old mayor, the 50-year-old retiree, the 65-year-old father of a preschool child and the 70-year-old college student. When we think in fresh categories, we no longer say, 'Oh, you're too old . . . or too young . . . or not qualified to attempt that.' "

5. *Simplify your life in order to pursue your vocation.* Simplifying one's life is the most difficult thing in the world.

Pope John XXIII once said very wisely, "See everything, overlook most things, try and change a few things." Genius is to see it all, but to zero in on the one thing you want to do. The ability to simplify is the genius of good management or the management of your life or mine.

Evolution is invariably from the complex to the simple. Aircraft engineers began by making a very complicated piston engine for planes. That evolved to a propjet with fewer parts, then to a jet engine with even less parts and finally to the rocket with the fewest parts of all. If you have a genuine vocation—a calling—you need to simplify your life to accommodate that calling. For example, a homemaker who wants to become a concert pianist better clean the house less often and cook fewer gourmet meals. I suggest a little planned neglect in terms of the everyday job. You may not be able to pursue your vocation in addition to what you're doing now. Something may have to go. Make a decision to do those other things less often, that you may do more of the thing God has given you to do.

Sometimes I wish that by some miracle each of us would have the interest on $2 million for the rest of our lives. We'd be in the position of never having to make a living again. We could not hide behind the fact that we are trapped in some "dumb job." We would be forced to find out what we really want to do with our lives. We would be free to discover from God what our true calling is. To find your vocation is to find who you are.

6

You and Your Marriage

A wise man said that while life is one crazy thing after another, love is two crazy things after each other. This past year on Valentine's Day, I preached on marriage. It was a sermon not just for those who are married. It was for those who would someday be married, the young and hopeful and the older singles as well, who may marry for the first or second time. It was also for those who may never marry but who are called upon to help and counsel friends who are married. I had been asked by a number of people to say something about marriage from a biblical perspective. What is marriage? Why does it not work? How can it work?

My topic was "Marriage Can Be Fun." If it is, you might ask, then why are there are so many rotten jokes about marriage. For example, there is the mother whose daughter wanted to have a talk about marriage. "Dear," she said, "why don't you talk to your father. He knows more than I do. He made a better choice than I did." Or when two women met downtown, one remarked that she had been chasing all over town trying to get something for her husband. "Any offers?" asked her friend. Or, the lady in the grocery store who asked for a pound of grapes. "They are my husband's favorite. Have they been sprayed with poison?" "No, you've got to buy that in the drugstore," replied the grocer.

Then there's the man who was so desolate when his wife died that he went to a spiritualist who professed to be able to contact her. When the apparition appeared, he said, "Alice, is it really you? Are you happy?" She said, "Yes, John, I'm happy." "Are you happier than when you were married to me?" "Yes, John, I'm happier than when I was married to you." "Oh, heaven must be wonderful!" "Who said I'm in heaven?" Now those all happen to be husband jokes, but wife jokes abound as well—such as comedian Henny Youngman's famous line, "Take my wife . . . please!"

Why is it that some of the worst jokes that you and I have ever heard have to do with marriage? Perhaps we need to laugh to camouflage so much of the pain so many of us have felt or witnessed in marriage. Marriage *can* be fun but often it is anything but. I believe marriage is a gift of God, one of the great gifts that God has given to us. So what's our problem?

First let me suggest that getting married is not the great purpose of life. Isn't that good news? God did not create us and Christ did not redeem us so that we might be married.

Nevertheless, that is a mind-set that many of us still have, especially those of an older generation. My mother had this mind-set. She was a great Christian saint but she never failed to use every opportunity to tell any one of her three grandchildren, "I'm praying that you'll get married." A couple of years ago our only daughter, then in law school, was in love with a student for the ministry. This news thrilled my mother. "Wouldn't she make a wonderful minister's wife?" was her comment. I said, "Yes, Mother, I think she would. But the question they're debating right now is whether or not he would make a good lawyer's husband." She was thunderstruck. Such a situation was beyond her imagination. My mother really felt that the goal of life was to be married, especially for a female.

I think a lot of people in the past have felt that way. As I said, I believe marriage is a gift, one that can help you be more whole. It's like the gift of health. There are many physically handicapped people in the world who may never be whole in this life, who are nonetheless sounder than a lot of us who are physically healthy. Health is a great gift, but lack of health in some area does not keep you from being a whole person. Marriage, like health, is a gift. It enhances life but it is not the reason for life.

Celibacy also is a gift. The Bible makes this very clear. Paul spoke about it. He said, "Listen, if you have the gift of celibacy, rejoice. If you can live without marriage, life can be better for you" (*see* 1 Corinthians 7:8). Who, for example, would dream of saying of someone like Mother Teresa, "Isn't it too bad that woman never got married." She is living life to the hilt. I've talked to a number of single people in my own parish who are saying, "I haven't time to get married. God has me in too many exciting things right now."

I had a remarkable godmother who was single all her life. She came to this country from Sweden as a penniless little girl who could't speak English. In one lifetime, she was a nurse, a hospital administrator, a doctor, and an ophthalmologist. She earned advanced degrees in higher mathematics and in law. Men chased this big, beautiful blonde lady all over Chicago. But Dr. Olga had no time for marriage. Her life was full. She spent two-thirds of her time caring for the poor, treating those who couldn't pay for medical services. She wasn't against marriage; it simply would have interrupted the exciting work she was involved in.

But some of you are like me, and I discovered early on that I don't have the gift of celibacy. The Bible gives us comforting words, "Better to marry than burn" (*see* 1 Corinthians 7:9). You see, the whole issue is put into proper perspective. If you don't have the gift of celibacy, the Bible advises that you look for the right person and let God bless you with the gift of marriage. But make no mistake about it, life is not made for marriage.

What is the purpose of marriage from the biblical point of view? I think marriage at best is a creative union that produces a synergy, which means that the whole is greater than the sum of the parts. In marriage, one plus one should equal much more than two, and I don't mean children.

Two people who don't have the gift of celibacy find fulfillment in marriage. Marriage is a sacrament. Each of you becomes a physical, visible expression to your spouse of God's unconditioned love. When you've been so bad, or rotten, or selfish that you can't believe God loves you, along comes your spouse and loves you when you least deserve it. This is a little taste of how God loves you. In marriage you become expressions to each other of God's love.

When I preached on marriage, I chose a text from the second chapter of Genesis. "And the man and his wife were both naked, and were not ashamed" (Genesis 2:25 RSV). I think the congregation was expecting a naughty sermon. But the nakedness described in this story of Adam and Eve has little to do with physical, sexual nakedness. It means they were hiding nothing from each other. They were simply two people who had no secrets. Each was known by the other and they were not ashamed. They enjoyed being who they were in the presence of the other and in the presence of God, who walked with them daily in the Garden. At its best, marriage is the means by which you are totally exposed before someone else and you're not ashamed. You come to know who you are, to accept yourself, and to experience God's love through the other person.

Since I've been back in the parish, I've had the opportunity to do a good deal of premarital counseling. Couples want to know what makes a good marriage, a fulfilling relationship. I suggest at least four things. The first is a common goal. Saint-Exupéry said once, "Love does not consist of gazing at each other, but of looking outward in the same direction." It's a triangular relationship. Two people are not focused on each other, but on a common goal. For Christians who love each other that outward focus is not on something but on someone: Jesus Christ the Lord of Life. A common goal is essential for any good marriage, and for a Christian marriage this goal is Christ Himself.

But a common goal is not all that is necessary for a fulfilling marriage. Sexual attraction—romance—is essential. If you don't feel that mysterious, undefinable emotion for this particular person, the relationship probably can't work. God has put this sexual hunger in us, and if you don't feel that for the other person, there will be hard and lonely years ahead. Next is the whole matter of friendship. Friendship is the daily bread of the relationship. Two people who really enjoy each other, who can sit and talk night after night and never run out of things to say, two people who can be off alone in some cabin in the woods and never tire of each other, those two people are going to make it. Sam Levenson once said, "Love at first sight is no miracle; it's love when you've been together 30, 40, or 50 years." If you are in the other person's company 30, 40, or 50 years and still say, "Wow, isn't he/she neat"—that's the miracle.

Finally, I believe respect is fundamental for a good and lasting marriage. Marriage ought to create a climate where respect for yourself and for the other person grows. Each person becomes more in the presence of the other. This is synergy. Listen to what "contemporary theologian" Clint Eastwood said about the man-woman relationship. Since you might say he's something of a sex symbol, his remarks are singular. "I think men want the same things as women. They want a woman who can rise to any occasion, a woman who has grace under pressure, who can be counted on. There is more to a relationship than sex." And I say, "Amen!" What we want, each of us, is a spouse we respect, someone whose behavior is reliable, whose integrity we can depend on.

These are the four ingredients of a good marriage that I discuss with engaged couples. Even with all four present it's hard enough to make a marriage work. The absence of any one can cause marriage to seriously flounder. It's hard to have a creative relationship if you have goals that simply do not mesh. One partner may say, "Money is important to me. I was so poor as a child that I need the security of money." If the other partner doesn't care about money, there is bound to be conflict. If your goal is some kind of social status, to be sought after by important people—the mayor, governor, whatever—you'd better choose a spouse who is comfortable with that. If you're a Christian for whom God is the most important thing in life and you marry someone who is not a Christian, you have a hopeless situation. The Bible advises us clearly against this and not because of some theological snobbery. If the center of your life is God Himself and your spouse says, "God who?" there is no possibility for a creative relationship.

One of the primary causes of marital breakdown, I think, is a lack of openness. We start to have secrets. Not just major secrets—robbing a bank or committing adultery—but the little secrets of life. We start withholding those times during the day when we behaved badly, handled things poorly. We don't tell our spouse and the first thing we know we're on guard. Our behavior becomes reserved, controlled, and rigid, and psychologists tell us that's what leads to a boring marriage. When there are enough little secrets between us, we are no longer spontaneous, and a nonspontaneous marriage, where both are playing a role, is a dull marriage. So, being open, naked, and unashamed about the good and the bad that happens day by day is essential to an exciting marriage.

Marriage can break down when we expect it to provide total security. We are afraid of risks. We use the marriage as a hiding place, a place to keep from facing life. We can run from the world to the safe arms of our lover and spouse. J. Lemaitre said, "Using another as a means of satisfaction and security is not love. Love is never security. Love is a state in which there is no desire to be secure; it's a state of vulnerability." Well I believe God called us to risk, and that to be fully alive we need to be risking. In a successful marriage we encourage each other to be more risking in terms of caring and involvement.

Finally, I think a lot of marriages break down because of our unwillingness to face ourselves. Marriage is the great mirror. I had a long lunch this week with another pastor, and we began talking about our marriages. We decided that the most devastating thing about marraige, even to the person of our choice with whom we're still in love, is that it reveals our own rottenness. I think I'm a neat guy until I get married and all my shortcomings are revealed. I say, "I couldn't have done that. I couldn't have said that." My wife says, "But you did." Living day after day, year after year, with somebody who is a kind of magnifying mirror, I see who I am and it's painful. For some it's so painful they say, "I've got to get out of this marriage. You've turned me into this unlovely person." But marriage changes nobody.

Marriage reveals who we are and if we can't bear to see who we are, we may be driven to terminate the marriage and perhaps find someone else . . . someone who is a better prop for our scenario. We marry someone who is dumber than we so we will look smart. We marry somebody who has a serious mental or emotional problem. They become our project, and by comparison we look stable and rational. We marry a non-Christian so we can be the spiritual one. Or, we marry somebody younger so we can appear younger. The other person becomes a prop to make us look good instead of that mirror which relentlessly underscores who we really are.

Can you accept who you are? If you can't, don't get married, friends. Remember, God has accepted who you are and has loved and forgiven you.

How do we make our marriage work in terms of some specifics? There's the whole issue of authority—who's in charge? We're all playing power games, especially in marriage. My wife says, "What dress shall I wear tonight to the party, the green or the blue?" I used to say, "I don't care." Now, I realize it's an important question. I think about it and say, "Why don't you wear the green dress?" Imagine my surprise when she emerges in half an hour wearing the blue dress. She always has an explanation, "I don't have the right shoes for the green one, and so forth." I'm beginning to be a little aware of her game. Of course, I'm not nearly so aware of my own. But each partner is guilty of this sort of thing. The big issue is not what we do, it's who decides what we do.

Marriage can become a power struggle. Power turned sour has been the human problem since the Garden of Eden. Who's in charge? A lot of conservative Christians think they have this all solved when they quote Ephesians 5:22, "Wives be submissive to your husbands." They ignore what follows, which is that the husband is to love his wife as Christ did the church. And He gave up His rights, and indeed His life, for the church. That's ultimate submission. The power struggle can only be resolved as each of us submits to the other and to God. There is no hierarchy of authority apart from that. A healthy marriage is not founded on some chain of command (contrary to what is being taught in popular national seminars just now). It's not a hierarchy, it's two people before Christ, equal partners in the game of life, submitting to each other. "In Christ," Paul says, "there is neither male nor female but a new creation" (*see* Galatians 3:28).

How about sexual fidelity? The devil would have us believe that God disapproves of sex, and therefore He doesn't want us to mess around. Actually, sex is one of the best gifts God has given the human race. Because it is so powerful, He does not want us to misuse it. Find one person, invest yourself in that person for life, and you become one flesh with that person. If you become one flesh with two or three or four people, your own personhood is jeopardized, you become "schizophrenic." You don't know who you really are. Sex, far from being sinful and evil, is the means by which union and communion at the deepest level is possible. If you don't have the gift of celibacy, then marry and commit yourself to sexual fidelity. In terms of premarital sex, let me say that in my years of counseling I've never met a couple who said to me, "We are sorry we waited to have sex 'til after we were married." Nobody is sorry they waited. Many are sorry they jumped the gun. In His wisdom, God requires sexual purity before and during marriage because it is in our own best interests.

In any relevant discussion of marriage today we must also deal with the issue of divorce. What about divorce? A lawyer in San Francisco said, "There are two processes that should not be started prematurely—embalming and divorce." Is divorce the unforgivable sin? Of course not. Is divorce acceptable? Sometimes. It can be the lesser of two evils. Sometimes, because of the hardness of our hearts, it is the only possible solution. Let's not make divorce *the* great sin. It's one of many sins; all sins are bad. We are frail people, and sometimes we must get out of a marriage for survival. None of my Christian friends who are divorced are promoting divorce. They admit their failure and they believe in a God who can forgive failure.

But what are some of the ways we can behave to avert the final tragedy of divorce? I think you must first of all ask the question, "Do I really want this marriage to work?" If you do, if you still love your partner, then make that love negotiable. Love in terms that your partner understands. Say it and act it out. Affirm the other person in every possible way. Take every opportunity to convey the message, "Boy, am I lucky to have you!" in word and deed. Don't be like the old Vermonter who after fifty years of a joyless, juiceless marriage, finally said to his wife, "Dear, you know some days I love you so much I have all I can do to keep from telling you."

Perhaps you're discouraged about your marriage because of frequent and violent quarrels. Remember, anger is not the opposite of love. Anger and love are two sides of the same coin. Indifference is the opposite of love. Don't be afraid of anger and conflict but learn to fight fairly. Stick to the issue at hand. Don't start reviewing mistakes of yesterday or five years ago. Let the other person have the freedom to be angry. Don't withdraw or insist on your own innocence.

I continue to believe that marriage is one of God's good gifts to us, but it's not for everybody, and no one need feel that he or she has to be married. As we said earlier, marriage will not solve your problems. Your marriage is not what's wrong with you, and changing spouses will not solve your personality problems. *You* are what's wrong with you. The Bible is clear on that. Marriage can be fun. When it is not, then we have missed the good thing God had in mind for us.

7

You and Your Journey

I wonder if you can say honestly that you really enjoy a long trip with your family in the family car. Someone has said, "Traveling with children is always traveling third class." I think most of us have mixed feelings about traveling with the family.

Let me tell you about a family trip we took about fifteen years ago when our three kids were small. It was to be the trip of a lifetime—a six-week-long journey from New Jersey all through the South, down into Mexico, back up the West Coast as far as Seattle and then home across the continent by the northern route. We started out in July in an unair-conditioned Volkswagen bus. We were five in all, plus one neurotic dog, a springer spaniel with very long hair, which was shedding and blowing around that car for six whole weeks. Actually Duke, the dog, had a nervous breakdown on the trip and never really recovered. He was partly cata-tonic the rest of his life. We had bought a tent especially for this trip—a great, big pyramidal tent—and out of deference to my wife and daughter we got one with a bottom in it in the event of bugs or snakes. On the first night of camping out, somewhere in the Carolinas, our dog relieved himself in the tent. It was never the same again.

I can remember scenes of endless fighting. The three kids in the back seat argued constantly about who did what and why. I'd like to forget the many times I drove at sixty miles an hour with my left hand on the wheel, my eyes straight ahead on the road, and my right hand reaching back, swinging furiously, trying to punch somebody, anybody, yelling, "Stop it. Quit it. Don't do that anymore!" I particu-larly remember the afternoon we reached the Grand Can-yon. We had saved for years for this trip, and there we were coming to one of the all-time biggies—the Grand Canyon. "Children, look," I cried, "There is the Grand Canyon." They'd look up from their Walt Disney comic books and say, "Very nice," and go back to Uncle Scrooge and Donald Duck. I'd say, "Listen, you're here to look at the Grand Canyon. You could have read those comic books at home."

One special memory is of running out of gas in Mexico out in the middle of nowhere. We just sat for hours until fi-nally an old peasant came along and siphoned some gas out of his battered truck into our car. He wouldn't even take any money. He just said, "No, glad to help." I remember driving across the Mojave Desert on a two-lane, no-passing highway behind a truck full of dead cows going to a rendering plant.

We spent two hours behind that truck in 120-degree temperatures, going about thirty-five miles an hour. Then there was the night when, arriving in Portland to visit friends, I asked the kids to get the dog and put him in the backyard. There was no dog. We had left him at a gas station 100 miles back.

These are some of my memories of our once-in-a-lifetime trip. But believe it or not, when our family gets together now as five adults, that trip is one of the great events in our memory bank. We reminisce at length and always end up saying, "Wasn't that a great trip!" And somehow it's true. Why is that? I think it's partly because a trip like that is a unique means of discovering something about ourselves and about each other. Traveling with somebody else reveals a lot about the person we are—our resources, our disposition, our habits. We learn good things and bad things. It's a short course in self-awareness. We learn things about the people with us, good and bad, and usually we end up feeling closer to each other. In spite of the catastrophes, accidents, and difficult times, somehow the five Larsons and that poor dog came closer together. And I think most of all we discovered that God was adequate for our mistakes, our shortcomings, our bad tempers. God was there in tangible ways blessing us.

I believe God has a journey in mind for all of us. I'm convinced that whenever God wants to do something new or teach us something, He takes us on a trip. There is no better way to reveal Himself to His faithful people than to get them on the road traveling with Him. That's what He did with the

Israelites when He brought them out of Egypt. For forty years God traveled with His faithful people. They left Egypt and wandered in the Sinai Peninsula, which is something like the Mojave Desert, where there was almost no water and no vegetation.

A friend of mine in Chicago, Dr. Robert Charnin, did his dissertation on the logistics of that trip. He came up with certain statistics by using the Book of Numbers plus present day computations. He has estimated that 3,600,000 people left Egypt. Seventy Israelites went there originally, and if they stayed 420 years and doubled their number every 25 years, that would be the size of the group making the Exodus. If every family had an average of 2 sheep, 1 cow, 1 camel, and 1 donkey, that would add up to 7 animals per family, or about 3,600,000 animals. He tells us that if those people plus animals marched 50 abreast there would be a line 123 miles long.

Dr. Charnin has also estimated the supplies needed for that group. Let's say that in the desert you would use 1 gallon of water per person per day and 2 gallons per animal. It would require 1,080 railroad tank cars of water a day to keep them going. Then there's the manna. There was no food and God supplied anew each day that kind of frosty, protein substance that forms on the rock. The animals and the people survived on that for 40 years—no Big Macs, no Kentucky Fried Chicken. The actual meaning of the word *manna* is "What is it?" They were hungry and when God sent them manna that first morning, the people said, "What is it?" And they ate "What is it?" for 40 years. No home-cooked meals, no peanut butter. The manna required to feed the animals and the people would fill 160 boxcars a day.

In those 40 years the Israelites must have learned a lot about themselves and about God. In the midst of 40 years of births and deaths, God was sending 160 boxcars of manna and 1,080 tank cars of water into the desert daily. Most present-day Jewish theology comes out of the recorded history of what God did on that incredible journey and it's no wonder. Bear in mind that all of us who are Christians are Jews as well. The Exodus is an important part of our history.

God revealed Himself to the people in this journey for forty years until a whole new generation was ready to inhabit the Promised Land. But after they had left Egypt and gone through the Red Sea (and, by the way, marching fifty abreast at two and a half miles an hour, it would take forty-nine hours to cross), God spoke these words as they began this journey. "Now therefore, if you will obey my voice and keep my covenant, you shall be my own possession among all peoples; for all the earth is mine, and you shall be to me a kingdom of priests and a holy nation" (Exodus 19:5,6 RSV). God was saying that it might take a journey of forty years for them to discover that the earth is His, that they belonged to Him, that they are a family, a nation of priests and blessers. Within those forty years He revealed Himself as someone able to take care of all their needs. The Exodus is one of the great trips in all history because God revealed to us who we are and who He is.

God has always had His people on a journey. Abraham wandered most of his life from Ur down to the Palestinian area. Jesus, when He began His ministry, took twelve people on a three-year journey. He must have considered that the fastest way for them to discover who they were personally, who they were as a family, who Jesus was and who God is. Saint Paul was an itinerant missionary, always on a journey. In *Pilgrim's Progress* John Bunyan paints life as a pilgrimage, suggesting that we Christians are on the way, moving from here to someplace else. All of this seems to point out that a journey is the best means of revealing who we are, our strengths and weaknesses, our faith or lack of it.

We Christians are all on a journey. The Bible reminds us that we are traveling toward that city not built with hands but eternal and made by God. The city in which we live can be some kind of pale foreshadowing of that Eternal City, and those cities that we dwell in for a time ought to be different because we are traveling to the City Eternal in the Heavens. And so faith is motion forward. Faith is not just simply what you say or what you believe. Thomas Carlyle said years ago, "If you do not wish a man to do a thing you had better get him to talk about it. For the more men talk the more likely they are to do nothing else." That's why we need to do more than to sit around and preach and talk and think and study about the faith. Faith requires that we move out for forty years or three years or even three weeks. We are in motion because God is out in front calling us to be in motion. Identity comes from direction. We learn who we are as we begin to move forward.

Katherine Anne Porter writes in her book *Ship of Fools,* "I'm appalled at the aimlessness of most people's lives today; fifty per cent don't pay any attention to where they are going; forty per cent are undecided and will go in any direction; only ten per cent know what they want, and even all of them don't go toward it." Terrible things happen to people, she says, like those in *Ship of Fools,* and they don't learn by it. They go into their graves the same shapeless creatures they were in their cradle.

God says to us as He did to the people of the Exodus, "Get up and get moving. I will go with you. You will be a Nation of Priests. You will learn who you are and you will learn who I am." For years I had a sign in my office that said, "Life is not a problem to be solved, but an adventure to be lived." And that's what God is saying to us. Let's focus on the adventure before us as we move toward that invisible and eternal city.

8

The Dialogue of Faith

Shortly before his death, I saw Jack Benny on the Johnny Carson show. During the interview, he turned to Johnny and in his inimitable way said, "You know the other night I dreamed about God. He said to me, 'Jack' ... (and he stopped with that characteristic long pause) You know, He knows *practically* everybody." It is mind boggling to realize that we have a God who is on a first-name basis with each one of us. Beyond that, He wants to spend time with us and talk to us.

What kinds of things do you think God wants to say to you in those quiet moments when you are lying on your bed at night or walking out under the stars? In one sense, you are what you think about when you are alone. What do you do when there is no distraction and when you are all by yourself? Where does your mind wander? Perhaps the thing we think of most often in those times is what we really worship. To be a Christian means that much of the time when we're alone, all by ourselves, our minds go to God and we talk to Him and He calls us by name and we have a dialogue. That's at the very heart of the Christian life.

In the Old Testament, we read about King David, former shepherd boy. David was someone who talked with God and with whom God talked. David was a sinful man, we know, but he was a man who was comfortable with God, who talked often to Him and listened to Him. We don't know exactly what God said to David in all those conversations, but I'd like to suggest that perhaps in those many times of dialogue, God might have asked David three basic questions—the same three He continues to ask us as we are in dialogue with Him today.

First of all, I'm sure God asked David repeatedly, "David, do you love me?" David might have answered by saying, "Wow, do I love You, Lord. I think about You all the time while I'm out there alone watching my father's sheep. Haven't I written You 150 love letters?" We still have the love letters David wrote to God, those psalms that say, "God, thank You." Or, "Why, God?" Or, "God, deliver me from my enemies." But he wrote all those letters to God. He could answer God's question with a resounding yes. And David's love letters to God became a witness to his love for thousands of years to come.

God's question is an eternal one. He says to you and me, "Jane or Tom, do you love me?" You may qualify your answer. You can say, "I hope You know I love You, Lord.

Much of the time when I'm alone my thoughts do turn to You, though not all the time. I complain to You when things do not go well. But I thank You for my health. I ask You to bless my neighbors and friends. I talk to You while driving on the freeway or while I'm walking the dog at midnight. Most Sunday mornings I can't wait to get to church to see Your people, to hear the music, to hear Your word, to be a part of the New Israel."

But I think God asks a second question that is an extension of the first. Perhaps God said to David, "Do you trust Me? Do you trust Me in the real world? It's one thing to trust Me as you sit alone watching the sheep and composing love songs, but do you trust Me where the rubber hits the road, where life is real and earnest?" What was the real world for David? He didn't have to contend with traffic jams or rising costs or income taxes, but he had to deal with the predators that attacked him and his sheep—the wolves, lions, bears. In those crises David could say, "Lord, I trust you. I go after those rascals with my slingshot because I believe You are there, and You have helped me many times to defend my father's sheep."

To those of us who have said we love God, God asks us that second question, "Do you trust Me? You love Me, but do you really trust Me?" We may say, "Lord, I trust You to save my soul. I trust You to forgive my sins. But can I trust You with my money? I'm not sure. You don't know the problems I have with money. You don't know about double-digit inflation. You don't know about having children in college and high tuition costs. How can I trust You with my money?" David needed to trust God for protection against lions and bears. Not being rural shepherds, our bears and lions take a different shape. We're out of work; can we trust God to find the right job at the right time? Can we trust Him with our budget? As students, can we trust Him with exams? Can we trust Him with the place where we're defeated, with the thing that keeps us awake at night?

I have a hard time with this. We moved to Seattle leaving an unsold home in Florida. We had a six-month grace period before we had to make final payment on the house we had bought. We were ten days short of the deadline before we had an offer on the Florida home. I confess that for part of that period I was not always trusting. On that red-letter day, it was as if the Lord said, "Do you think I had forgotten where you are? I have a road map to Seattle. I know where there's a couple who will be as thrilled to live in that Florida house as you were. Did you not trust me?" Mostly I did but I'm sure glad He came through.

Can you really believe that you can trust God with selling houses, buying houses, accepting a job, changing jobs, with your income and your budget? If God is Who He says He is, you need not be anxious. Can you really believe that? Our money is perhaps the ultimate test of our trust—and, of course, a job or no job directly affects our income. Exams are a prelude to that job. So when God asks us to trust Him, a good place to begin is with our money.

I remember a young dentist from a former parish who was struggling with the idea of tithing. He met with a small group of men on Saturday morning for prayer and Bible study. They belonged to a number of different local churches. We talked about our lives and prayed for each other. It was the time of year when most of our churches were observing Stewardship Sunday and we were all discussing money and giving. Some of the men were talking about the joys of tithing. "Listen," one said, "I'm a tither and I have never for a moment regretted giving one-tenth of what I have to the Lord for His work." This young dentist protested, "Listen, brothers, you have no idea how much money I'm presently making. I'm at the peak of my career just now, and I can't afford to tithe. Ten years ago I might have but now I'm making it big, and do you know what a tithe would be for me?" There is an old saying that when someone gets rich, that person either becomes God's partner or loses his or her soul.

A number of years later I was in touch with a very well-to-do young man who was a successful baker. As an act of trust in God, he put his bakery business in a five-year trust, during which time he could not receive any income. He said, "My wife and I want to live by faith in God for these next years. We want to learn what it's like to really trust God for our very existence." Now I don't particularly recommend that course of action. But this man felt that unless he had nothing and could still trust God, he was not sure he trusted Him at all.

In the New Testament, we read about Zacchaeus, the tax collector, and his remarkable conversion in the whole area of money. He had climbed a tree to watch Jesus and the disciples go by. Jesus saw him, asked him to come down, and

suggested he host a luncheon for the whole group. A tax
collector in those days was a despised person who sold out
his own people to collect taxes for Rome. Zacchaeus came
down and took Jesus to his home for dinner, and the love of
God overwhelmed him. The first thing he says after his remarkable transformation is: "Lord, half of what I have I
would give to the poor." He was saying, "I love you, I trust
you enough to give up the security of trusting in money."

In my growing-up years, my father managed the money
in our family. That was not difficult since we had none. We
were always behind on the rent and car payments. Our
clothes were threadbare. In short, we were Depression poor.
My father died while I was in the army in World War II. My
mother immediately suggested that we tithe. She asked my
opinion. I wasn't a Christian but I said, "Sure. Do what you
want." She began with whatever we had. I sent her an allot-
ment from the army. She had a job at Marshall Field's, and
she also took in roomers in her Chicago apartment. One-
tenth went to the Lord and from that time forward that little
widow began to prosper. However, her philosophy of tithing, which she expounded all too often, was somewhat em-
barrassing. She would say, "You know, I would tithe even if
I weren't a Christian. It's just good business." I would try to
point out that she seemed to have missed the point. She
would say, "If I didn't believe in God at all, I would tithe
because tithers prosper."A theological student by then, I
would say in chagrin, "Mother, that's the wrong reason for
tithing." I don't guarantee as my mother did that every

tither will prosper, but I do believe that when you can give all of your income, beginning with a significant portion, to God, He says, "Now, we're partners. You need never really worry again. I will take care of you."

I heard about a very wealthy Christian businessman who was asked back to his church to speak to the Sunday school class he attended long years ago. The children were curious about this man now worth millions and asked him to tell how it all began. He said, "Well, it all began right here in this church. Those were hard times. I was a young man with no job and very poor. We had a guest preacher who said, 'Give your life and all that you have to Jesus and He will bless you.' I had $3.54 in my pocket. It was all I had in the world, and I put the whole thing in the plate. I gave my life to the Lord that day and He has blessed me ever since." He closed his talk with a time for questions, and the first hand up was that of a little boy in the front row. "Mister," he said. "Could you do it now?" Of course, that's the heart of the problem. The more we have to trust God with, the harder it is to trust Him.

The third and final question I believe God might have asked David is this one: "David, do you love Israel?" And David might have said, "Ah, loving Israel, the nation, Your people, that is really a problem. Rumor has it that we have a crazy king running our country who is subject to fits of depression and who drinks too much. How can I love an Israel ruled by such a king? Closer to home, there's my father and my brothers. They tend to pick on me. I'm not too fond of our rabbi either. All in all, there's a lot of corruption and injustice in Israel." God might have said, "David, Israel is Mine, My people. If you love Me you must love Israel." And while David might have had many good reasons for not loving Israel, he nevertheless said yes to this final question. "Yes, Lord, because I love You I love Israel."

You and I are the New Israel, the Body of Christ, the Christian Church. All Christians belong to the New Israel and God is asking us to love Israel. David was asked to prove his love for Israel in a specific way. There was a problem in Israel, a political problem. Unless they could defeat a great, enormous man named Goliath, the Israelites would be a slave people for a long time to come. The whole fate of the nation hinged on finding someone to stand up to Goliath, this great champion of the Philistines. Now David could have responded differently. He might have said, "Listen, who am I? I'm just a teenager. I didn't create these problems. People older than I built this Israel and made this man king. They have gotten us into this mess. How can you expect me, a teenage boy, to volunteer to deliver this nation from the sins of the fathers?" But God's requirements were clear, "Because you love Me you must love Israel." And David sought out King Saul and offered to take on the giant, armed only with five small stones. Actually, he used just one. He loved God, trusted Him and was committed to fight for God's people.

Are we committed to love Israel, the New Israel? This is a problem we face in all of our churches. Each Sunday we find ourselves sitting in the pews beside some of the church's biggest problems. This is what the church is all about. We are a problem people who believe God loves us and has given us a destiny and called us to extraordinary things. God continues to ask us if we love Him. I think most of us do. Do we trust Him? A good many of us do. Do we love His church? That may be the hardest question of all.

9

You and Your Country

I have a confession to make. A few months ago I took a trip that resulted in the rekindling of an old love affair. I fell in love with my country all over again. Hazel and I spent a week in Texas visiting my old friend Keith Miller and his wife, Andrea. We decided to spend three of those days at the Mexican border town of Laredo. Gastronomically, it was a glorious time. Keith and I are both afficionados of Mexican food. And while we stayed in a hotel on the United States side, we commuted back and forth for meals in Nuevo Laredo. We ate everything and anything Mexican—enchiladas, tostados, tortillas, tacos, chiles rellenos and even goat (which I discovered is delicious). I should add that all this was consumed along with great draughts of Alka Seltzer. For three days we feasted as if there were no tomorrow.

Our hotel room overlooked that mysterious little river

called Rio Grande, which in some seasons runs fairly rap-
idly, as it did then, and which is almost nonexistent at other
times of the year. We were looking out at the world's most
traveled international border. There is more traffic, both
legal and illegal, between Mexico and the United States
than between any other two countries in the world. Our
view encompassed both sides of the river, and I could perceive no particular geographic differences. It is a desert area
on both sides and was greener than usual at that time, due to
recent rains. The climate is the same on both sides of the
river. Even the people look much the same.

And yet it is not the same. Those on the south side of the
river are doing everything in their power to cross to the
north side, as we said, through both legal and illegal means.
Two "kingdoms" exist side by side, and one offers a way of
life for which many are willing to risk all they have and
sometimes their lives. These invisible kingdoms are separated by an arbitrary, geographical boundary called the Rio
Grande. Many who cross that boundary settle down in the
immediate area in a place with identical geography and climate. But because they are in the United States, they are in
a vastly different environment, economically, politically,
and socially.

Those three days on the banks of the Rio Grande gave me
a new appreciation for this unusual country of ours. Since
then I have been asking myself just what is America? Our
government, though imperfect and sometimes corrupt, is
nevertheless the best government in the history of the world.
But any attempt to describe our nation would include more

than our system of government. How would you describe what America is? What symbolizes America for you? It may be the family gatherings and remembered holidays: Thanksgivings and Christmases, weddings and graduation ceremonies, and all the warm memories of family life in this great land. It may be Fourth of July celebrations with fireworks, homemade ice cream, lemonade on the front porch. You may associate America with the pilgrims who left their houses and lands in Europe and crossed a great ocean in small boats in order to worship God freely. Certainly the essence of America was caught by those signers of the Declaration of Independence in 1776. The dream was preserved by a bloody civil war, one which ensured that all citizens might be free and equal. The present America represents wealth, political power, and human and material resources such as no past king or emperor ever possessed.

For some citizens, America is the Indianapolis 500, the Super Bowl, and the World Series. We may think that would be a small minority, but during the baseball strike of 1981 a Mr. Allen of the *New York Post* wrote: "There is a tremendous emptiness in the land without baseball. Its absence creates a great void." A lot of us probably never noticed that void, but we are a "sportsaholic" nation. For some, America is baseball and spectaculars and super bowls.

But beyond all these possible descriptions of our nation, we who are Christians are seeking to find a biblical perspective on our relationship to our country and our responsibility to it. Have we any reason to believe that this land we love and belong to was and is and will be especially blessed of

God? Certainly, compared to South and Central America, we seem especially blessed in terms of freedom, prosperity, opportunity. One somewhat naive theory claims that this is the result of the fact that in the beginning North America was settled by believers seeking God and freedom of worship, while South America was discovered by soldiers seeking gold. Actually, there has been a great deal of debunking of those noble and honorable ancestors of ours in recent years. We are told that George Washington padded his expense account. Ben Franklin was a notorious womanizer. Thomas Jefferson had a mistress and kept slaves until the day he died. Present-day historians tell us our great founding fathers (and mothers) were fallible people.

It seems to me that the establishment of a just and free society is not particularly the product of any innate goodness. Rather it is the product of a motivating dream. The early pilgrims had a dream. The patriots during the revolution had a dream. The writers of our Constitution had a dream. They dreamed of a land where there was freedom and liberty based on equality under God.

And yet the dreamers who shaped our land were a minority. Historians tell us that the original thirteen colonies represented about 3 million people. Ninety percent lived in rural areas and were farmers. The largest city was Boston with 40,000 people. The war was fought over a territory of no great significance. At the time of the Revolution, only one-third of the population were patriots. About one-third were loyalists, who fought against their neighbors to preserve their ties with England and King George. One-third were indifferent and cared about neither cause. When we read of the terrible winter at Valley Forge with Washington's starving, freezing, poorly clothed army, we tend to assume all the colonists were caught up in a similar sacrificial effort. Actually, only a minority of the population was so involved. As we said, one-third were conducting "business as usual" and another third were against the whole enterprise. When we celebrate our independence each Fourth of July, let's remember we are honoring a small minority, those with a dream, who were trying to bring into being something that had never been before and which they believed was of God. America is, and continues to be, a fragile dream of a visionary minority.

During World War II, President Franklin Roosevelt said, "Religion and democracy stand and fall together." It's a lovely sentiment, but totally false. Christianity existed for seventeen hundred years before there was an America. Christianity existed and flourished under the Caesars, under feudalism, under tyrants of all sorts. Christianity exists quite apart from whether there is or is not a democracy. And yet there is a linkage between the two. I believe the democracy we have in the United States is the product and fruit of a spiritual dream that was inspired by God.

All of this leads us to the crucial question. What is the relationship of Christian faith and patriotism? Are they synonymous? Are they mutually exclusive? Exactly where is the true allegiance of the Christian, in terms of his or her homeland? If, first of all, we believe Jesus Christ is our Lord, then we have given Him our allegiance, our hearts, and our lives.

We belong to a Kingdom not of this world, but to the Kingdom of God. Our ultimate, all-pervasive loyalty is to that Kingdom. We are given to each other as a family, brothers and sisters to the world, because of our allegiance to this King. Given that premise, what is our relationship to the temporal kingdom we are presently a part of—our nation?

I meet a good many Christians who take the extreme position that America is the New Israel, God's chosen land. We, like Israel of old, are to bring God's justice and mercy and love to the world. They say, proudly, "My country, right or wrong." America and God are one and the same. There's another group of Christians who have copped out entirely in their desire to be otherworldly. They say, "Because my allegiance is to a higher cause, to the Kingdom of God, I don't even vote. America and all nations are temporary and fleeting. Powers and principalities are irrelevant. Let the nations rage. The Second Coming is imminent. My citizenship is in heaven."

I happen to believe that God is concerned about the nations. The Old Testament records the history of Israel, the nation God brought into being, and to whom He gave His blessing. In the New Testament that blessing is extended to all faithful believers in every and any nation. And they have an allegiance to a Kingdom not of this world.

But we are faced with a paradox. The thirteenth chapter of Romans indicates unequivocally that Christians are to submit to those who govern, because a sovereign God has placed them in positions of authority. If they were not meant to be there, God would remove them. We Presbyteri-

ans particularly stress the sovereignty of God. God is ruler
of all things. If you don't like your rulers, blame God. It
would all seem to back up the idea of unquestioning allegiance to government. But the same chapter goes on to say
that the ultimate law that sums up the Ten Commandments
is to love your neighbor as yourself. So, in the same chapter
we have injunctions that in certain circumstances could be
totally contradictory.

The highest law is to love your neighbor. Sometimes loving your neighbor may require civil disobedience. Christians
are often in the forefront of civil disobedience. Historians
have called the American Revolutionary War a Presbyterian
revolution: so many Presbyterian divines, though preaching
the sovereignty of God, were urging and fomenting civil disobedience. There is a wonderful story told about a historic
church in New Jersey that was under attack by the British.
Patriots holed-up there were fighting fiercely when wadding
for their muskets gave out. At that point, the preacher began
to tear up the hymnals to make wadding—hymnals full of
songs by the prolific Isaac Watts. "Give 'em Watts, boys!"
was his battle cry, as they stuffed hymn pages into their
muskets and continued to fight and to win. The story is still
repeated with pride in that church and indicates the extent
to which we Presbyterians were committed to the revolution.

The Bible indicates we are to honor our leaders. But suppose your leader is Adolf Hitler, who urges you to hate your
neighbor if he or she is Jewish. Are you to be loyal to a government that is hunting down and destroying your neighbor? What if your leader is Idi Amin or President An-

astasio Somoza? But God is concerned about nations, because our nation, its climate of freedom or oppression, justice or tyranny, shapes who we are. Being an American makes you different than you would be had you been born into the same family with the same genes in some other nation. Somehow, being American, we have absorbed attitudes, patterns, expectations, both good and bad. But in the same way our nation draws her identity not just from the pilgrims and signers of the Declaration of Independence but from you and me. We are shaping our nation, for better or worse.

As Christians, you and I need to take responsibility for the character and the direction of our land. We may perceive that direction very differently. We may be followers of Jerry Falwell and his Moral Majority or we may be in sympathy with William Sloane Coffin on the extreme left. But the ultimate sin is to be uninvolved in the destiny, the course, and the character of our nation. We don't have the option of saying, "It doesn't matter." Anyone who is concerned about this nation's direction has my blessing, though I may not agree with the kinds of change being proposed.

When the signers of the Declaration of Independence put their names down on that document, they signed their own death warrants. The chances of success seemed frail, and had they lost, it would have cost their property and their lives. That little group of people, many of them devout Christians, bet their lives on a dream that they believed was of God. God does care about nations. He cares that you and I care about our nation. How can we be in God's will and be a blessing? I believe the key is servanthood. God blesses the nation that wants to serve Him—the nation that wants to go beyond serving its own interests and to become instead God's servant in the world. Now the United States of America would seem to be the most blessed and privileged nation now or ever. But the Old Testament provides a lesson for us as it records the story of Israel, the nation which had, and still has, a covenant with God unlike any other country. Even Israel was abandoned by God during times of disobedience. The covenant still stands, but God removed His blessing when Israel refused to be a servant nation.

In Proverbs 14:34, we read, "Righteousness exalts a nation, but sin is a reproach to any people" (RSV). God blesses the nation that exalts righteousness, and righteousness is far more than blue-stocking morality. We could ban all pornography and close all the saloons and still not be righteous. Certainly immorality is an affront to God and destructive to man, but righteousness is far more than morality. In the biblical view, the righteous nation will be just and compassionate and generous.

I was shocked when someone pointed out to me recently that Sodom and Gomorrah were not destroyed because of their open sexual immorality. In Ezekiel 16:49 we read, "Behold, this was the guilt of your sister Sodom: She and her daughters had pride, surfeit of food, and prosperous ease, but did not aid the poor and needy" (RSV). Sodom was destroyed because of its selfishness and indifference to the poor. God wants purity as best we can live it, but ultimately righteousness is love in action.

Love requires justice, compassion, mercy, and generosity toward all people, even the alien in our land. I was pleased to read that our 1981 General Assembly of the United Presbyterian Church appointed a committee to study our treatment of aliens. We are experiencing just now a wave of legal and illegal aliens coming across our borders, not just from Mexico but from Haiti, Cuba, Vietnam, Cambodia, and from all corners of the world. Illegal aliens have special problems. They are exploited by employers, and if discovered, they, not the employers, are arrested. They pay more taxes and receive less benefits than citizens. In Old Testament times, the stranger in the land was to have the same rights as the Israelites. The stranger was to be paid promptly and fairly for any work done. The stranger was to receive the full protection of the law. God held Israel accountable for the treatment of the stranger within their land. One place where we can begin to practice righteousness is to concern ourselves about the stranger—the legal or illegal alien within our land.

Righteousness is also no-pressure evangelism: evangelism that emphasizes the Good News that you are loved—that in Jesus Christ there is a God who knows your name—that you are not hopeless—that He is here and you can meet Him. Righteousness includes sharing Good News that blesses people. This is quite the opposite of forcing morality or doctrine on people. C. S. Lewis wrote, "Of all the tyrannies, the tyranny exercised for the good of its victims may be the most oppressive. It may be better to live under robber barons than under omnipotent moral busybodies. The robber baron's cruelty may sometimes sleep. His cupidity may at some point be satiated. But those who torment us for our own good will torment us without end. For they do so with the approval of their own conscience."

The righteous nation is not one full of moral busybodies. The righteous nation is peopled by those who are pouring themselves into the nation to bring about justice for the disinherited and the oppressed.

America is a tangible dream. I believe it is partly God's dream. America is also our corporate dream in which we need to invest our spiritual capital. A good many of this nation's wealthy old families have lived by the maxim, "Don't touch your capital." Rather, you were to live off the interest from all sorts of wise investments. Our land exists in its present state because in every generation a minority has invested its spiritual capital. By virtue of being born into this land, you and I begin to consume that capital. If we consume too much, the next generation will have little or none. I think we are to be those people who are investing spiritual capital that others may profit. God's people, a minority in the land, are called to produce capital for future generations.

The true patriot is one who is finding ways to increase the spiritual capital in this country, that neighbor might love neighbor, that justice might prevail, that mercy will flourish, that generosity and kindness will increase. To do less is to steal the birthright of future generations and to diminish our own.

10

Loving and Dreaming

Our youngest son was married last fall in Los Angeles, and our old friend Lloyd Ogilvie officiated. It was all upbeat until the point where he asked who was giving this beautiful bride away. In a barely audible and emotion-choked voice, her big, handsome stepfather said, "Her mother and I do." He sat down with tears flowing down his cheeks. My wife, Hazel, came prepared with a special crying handkerchief someone had made her just for the occasion. I tried to cry a little more discreetly.

But there was also much laughter and joy as God brought these two people together to belong to each other. At best this union will create a synergy that will bless many people in the years to come. But during the ceremony, in all the joy and tears, I was struck again by the familiar words of the wedding vows. "Do you take this man/woman, in sickness and in health, in joy and in sorrow, for better or for worse?" Sitting there, in a Presbyterian chapel in Los Angeles, participating in that wedding, I seemed to be hearing a fresh message about the high cost of loving. For loving, real loving, for better or worse, in sickness and health, is costly. In any relationship of love, marriage, friendship, or whatever, there is an enormous cost for each one.

In the marriage relationship, there is of course the possibility of children. I was appalled to read recently that the cost today of rearing a child through high school is $70,000. If that child goes on to college, the cost is over $100,000. That is the high cost of loving. There is a high cost in loving children apart from their material needs. Teachers pay a high price for loving as they go into the classrooms, whatever age group they teach—kindergarten, primary, high school, college. If it does not cost you something to be there, you are probably not giving it your all. We think of the enormous price a teacher like Annie Sullivan paid to reach the blind, deaf, mute Helen Keller. She persisted through her student's anger, hatred, and rebellion and fought her way into her life to call forth a gifted and unusual woman.

And God, Himself, paid a high cost to be our Lover, Father, Saviour, and Friend. In John 3:16, we read, "God so loved . . . that he gave his only begotten son . . ." (KJV). The high cost of loving for God meant watching His only Son be mocked, ignored, beaten, and finally killed by us. There is a high cost of loving for God's people. The bottom line is that we are to love one another as He has loved us. As God so loved the world, we must love the world.

A few months ago the director of an Episcopal retreat house near Toronto was telling me a story about some of his Mennonite neighbors. He said that at harvest time, they always stop off at his center on the way to market and leave one-tenth of all the produce in their carts. When the day is over, they come back and deposit all the fruits and vegetables that are not sold. The director once asked these Mennonites, "Why don't you save yourself a trip and just stop on the way back from market?" They were horrified at such a suggestion. "God says, 'Bring the first fruits,'" they explained, "not what's left over." Those Mennonite farmers understand the high cost of loving.

Mahatma Gandhi once said, "Even God does not dare to appear before a starving man except in the form of food." And if you and I are to be God's people, we go to those who are hungry and bring food. If we are God's people, we bring our first fruits and offer them to others. In 1503 Erasmus wrote to the church of his time: "A fellow member starves while you are belching the flesh of partridges. A naked brother shivers while your superfluous clothing goes to waste by moth and dry rot. Do you still think of yourself as a Christian when you are not even a man?"

And yet in all this there is a paradox. There is a high cost in loving and there is no cost at all. The Bible says that God loves the hilarious (cheerful) giver. God so loved that He gave His Son to be ignored, abused, mocked, tortured, and killed. And yet on that night when the angels proclaimed the birth of the Holy Child, they sang, "Good news to all men of good will." An omniscient God knew how costly His gift would be ultimately, but He paid the price joyfully.

Our son and his bride are living now in Florida, where he is a probation officer. Let's imagine that one night he comes home late from a difficult day to find that dazzling Florida moon coming up over the palm trees. They have had a special dinner by candlelight. Suddenly he moves close to her, leans over, smells her perfume, and begins to hold her in his arms. Do you suppose at that point he's thinking, "This may cost us $70,000"? Of course not. The cost is never even considered.

Do you remember the first time that you were in love? You may have been ten or fifteen or forty. The first time love really hit me hard I was a sophomore in high school. I was working as a stock boy for Marshall Field's in Chicago. I worked every afternoon after school and all day Saturdays, and in one month I had saved up enough to buy a Christmas present for a girl with whom I was passionately in love. My mother tried to dissuade me. "Are you sure you want to do this? You worked long and hard and that's a lot of money." I wanted to do it! Would you believe that I had never even kissed that girl and I still haven't. But I gave a month's wages to buy her a present and I did so joyfully. That was the high cost of loving, and to me it was no cost at all.

Some of you have parents who have worked and saved to provide for you and get you through college. If you had said, "I can't let you pay that price," you would have robbed them of a great gift. You gave them the gift of loving you and in real love there is no high cost. Think of someone like Mother Teresa. Do you think she is paying a high price for loving the poor of Calcutta? On the contrary, I think she'd say, "I'm where it's at." She implies that the rest of us are missing something.

If we are lovers of God, it follows that we are lovers of the world. There is a high cost to that love, but that cost is paid cheerfully. I saw a sign recently that said, "The Lord loveth a cheerful giver, but he also accepteth from a mean old grouch." Mean old grouch or cheerful giver, you can give and God will bless the gifts. If you begin to be a cheerful giver, you're not concerned about the high cost of loving.

But, love also requires a shared dream for the future. When two people fall in love, they begin to dream about their life together, their future home, and possible family, perhaps the meshing of careers. They begin to dream about taking their place in a church and being part of the people of God. Our lives are shaped by dreams—our own and the dreams others have for us, often our parents, sometimes a teacher or friend.

Some time ago I read a wonderful story about an artist who was painting some Old Testament prophets. He often went out into the streets to look for his models and one night he came upon an old wino, complete with white hair and a beard. He offered the man five dollars to come back to the studio and sit for a portrait. While the old derelict sat dozing in an alcoholic haze, the artist painted the Prophet Isaiah. When the artist finished, the drunk asked to see the portrait.

He was so astounded to see himself pictured as a noble Old Testament prophet that he left with these words, "I promise you and God that I will never drink again. I am going to become the man you saw sleeping here in your studio." The artist saw the invisible, and the invisible became the reality.

Dr. Karl Menninger, sage American psychologist, says that when you begin to see what you can become, your problems are mostly over. You cannot get well as long as you feel trapped in the old, a prisoner of the past, a victim of your track record. Change begins at the place where you can begin to dream about what you can become.

The Bible is full of stories of people with a dream. We read, "Where there is no vision, the people perish ..." (Proverbs 29:18 KJV). Abraham had a dream. He left the familiar and went out into the unknown to be a part of God's plan for the nation Israel, new and old. Paul had a dream. This fanatic Jew had a dream about Jesus and the Kingdom of God and set out to bring that dream to the world. Through Paul, God spread the Gospel through the Roman Empire. At one point, God intervened in his life by means of a specific dream. He had a choice of going to Asia or Europe and in the dream he saw a man from Macedonia who said, "Paul, come over here. We need you." And so the Gospel came to Europe—and hence to America. We American Christians are indebted to that vision that came to Paul and changed the course of his journey.

Jesus had dreams for His followers that must have amazed them. He told some ordinary, rough fishermen,

"Come, I will make you fishers of men." I am sure they
had a hard time believing that, but they went. Jesus had
a dream for Simon. He said to Simon, that blustery and
unreliable fisherman, "You're Peter (a rock). And on that
rock I will build my church." The Gospels give us countless
stories of Jesus sitting down with people one by one and
conveying His dreams for them and for the people they can
become.

Perhaps there was someone in your own life who was able
to communicate his or her dream for you and your poten-
tial. Can you remember the first person in your life who was
able to relate to you in such a way that you saw yourself in a
whole new light? It might have been a neighbor or an older
relative. It might have been a peer, a pal you hung around
with. But was there some one person along the way who was
able to give you a new picture of who you are? Those are
very special people—those who called forth something un-
discovered . . . and suddenly we became, and we are still becoming, the person they saw in us. This is a big part of our
ministry to each other.

Let me suggest to you that life is shaped either by our
dreams or by our problems. We can spend our lives problem
solving. We all do that too much of the time. We focus on
our problems. "I don't have a job. How can I get one?" Or,
"I don't like my job. How can I change it?" Or, "I'm single
and I want to be married. How can I find the right mate?"
Or, "I'm married and unhappy. How can I change that?"
Or, "I'm retired and I need something to do." Or, "I'm
overworked. How can I find more leisure time?" The prob-

lems of our lives, with money, sex, relationships, jobs, will never all be solved, and to focus entirely on them is a very dull and uncreative way to live.

God gives you another choice. You can live by His dreams for you by implementing those dreams. God can give you a dream for your life and for the places where you're involved, just as He did Abraham or the Apostle Paul. Suddenly you see something you want to do for Him. You have a vision for a ministry to a certain sector of society, a part of the church making a difference somewhere. You can be a person who implements that dream, making your job and your money and your resources fit into that dream. You may need to reshift your resources to implement the dream.

Two of our parishioners, Denny and Jeanne Grindall, go out for part of each year as missionaries to the Masai in Africa. They have helped this nomad people to build a lake and taught them to fish and grow crops (all of which are firsts for this tribe). Each year when they arrive in the village, the Masai say, "Denny, Jeanne, what are you dreaming about right now for us?" Last year they had a dream for a dam. The Masai were mystified, "A dam, what's that?" And so the work began as the Grindalls began to share their dream and the dream began to be implemented and become real enough to change the way the people live.

America right now is in desperate need of a new dream. We continue to focus on our problems with inflation, unemployment, the arms race, diminishing resources, endangered ecology. As a nation, we are focused on solving innumerable problems. And the thing we need most is a vision of what God has called our nation to be. Assuming God gives us a vision, we still have all kinds of problems, but they will be the problems inherent in implementing a vision of a new kind of America.

Long before I moved to Seattle, I was blessed by one of its native sons. His name was Abraham Vereide, and he came to Seattle years ago as a young Norwegian immigrant. This immigrant boy had two passions, one for Jesus and the other for America, which he believed was the land of opportunity and spiritual destiny. God gave Abraham Vereide a dream for reaching our nation's leaders. He was concerned that most nations in the world have an embassy in Washington, D.C., but there was none for Jesus and His Kingdom. If the smallest, tiniest nation has a base from which to lobby for its interests, why not a lobby for the Kingdom of God? So he went to Washington with that dream, and he founded an embassy for Jesus Christ called Fellowship House. The presidential prayer breakfast and the governors' prayer breakfasts are outgrowths of that embassy. One little immigrant boy in Seattle had a dream and though he is now dead, people are still walking around and living in that dream.

The local church must have a vision. As a new pastor, I am acutely aware of how easy it is to live our corporate church life merely solving problems. It can take all our time. The roof over the sanctuary leaks. The whole church facility is in serious need of repair and maintenance. We need more funds for our mission program. But, if our corporate life is geared to maintaining the building or raising more money, then we are living by problem solving. What we really need is a vision of what God is calling us to do and be as His people in our time. There is no church anywhere like us—and that's true of every church. Every church has a unique destiny at this time and place in history. If we can capture God's dream of what He is holding us accountable for, then building and staff and finances are all implementation for that dream.

All of us have problems, and we can live by those problems, or we can live by implementing the dream that God has for our lives. A year or so ago, God gave Hazel and me a dream for our lives. We prayed that He would send us where we could live out our dream for the church with a small group of people in these next years. He sent us to a small group of two thousand plus in a big city church. I would caution you to make sure you really want what you pray for, because you might get a lot more than you ask for. But my dream for this new church family is severalfold. I hope that we might discover in the coming years together that the best resources God has are in the people of God, not in the pulpit, not in the staff, not in our glorious ancient history, and not in the speakers we invite in to dazzle and charm us. Our real wealth is in the people God has gathered together right now in our church and your church.

Now that I have returned to the pastorate, my dream for our church in Seattle is that we can be a place of healing for all people. There are so many hurting people in our time for whom the professionals have no answer. But the church could be a place where the nonmedically ill could find health and hope. People are hurting for all kinds of reasons. But whatever the hurt, I wish the world could say of the church, "This is my place. These are my people. They will accept me as I am. Together we'll find God's answer."

Second, I dream that we will move beyond the church's walls to confront those outside with a new way to live. I dream that we will become salt and light and leaven and love in our city as we go about on the buses, the trains, and the highways, and in the offices, and schools and factories.

If you have a dream for your church, share it. If you have no dream, God can give you one. I believe that your dreams for your church are its most valuable asset. Be a steward of those dreams. God may be waiting for someone to dream your particular dream.

11

Giving Yourself Away—
In One-to-One Counseling

You are never more you than when you are helping another. Since I've been back in the pastorate, I find most of my hours are spent listening to people one to one. I hear about hurts, pains, and mistakes. I jokingly refer to myself as a garbage collector. Actually, that really is the most exciting part of my job. Preaching is hard work and provides very little feedback. Mostly I hear from those who disagree with me. Preaching is a kind of scattershot. The real fun of living out the Good News in terms of communication is on a one-to-one basis.

I think that's true for most of us, preachers or otherwise. We want to be able to let God use us in the lives of those around us, with friends and family members who are hurting or floundering or confused. There are few things more exhilarating than to be an instrument through which another person finds faith, direction, healing, or peace. With that in mind, let's talk about some of the things we can learn to be and do as we enter into these kinds of life-changing dialogues.

We might start with some of the things to avoid. We are not called by God to straighten people out. We are not called to make people sinless or "sinners emeritus." We have all heard the kind of message that implies that if we really find Jesus and receive His spirit or belong to a particular church, we will never sin again. But we are not called to make people perfect so that they will be "little Jesuses." We are not called to help people attain some victorious life. The Good News is better than that.

It is not our job to teach people. I think I've been hung up on that for a long time. Sometimes I think my job is to straighten out people's theology, their psychology, their morals, and their values. It's not. We in the church experience a mystery. There are pastors, elders, and deacons who have been in the church for years and years who still have all sorts of doctrinal hang-ups. They don't quite get it. Others come in as new Christians and in a matter of months are somehow wise in the things of God and the issues of life. It's unfair. You can be around seminaries, theologians, classes for years and never understand the faith clearly. Or you can come into the Kingdom suddenly and perceive truth at once. Jesus said, "If any man wills to do my will, he shall know the doctrine whereof I speak" (*see* John 7:17). The doctrines follow life-changing decisions.

Jesus tells us that if any man be in Christ he is a new being. That's a valid goal in terms of your one-to-one counseling—to enable the other person to become that new being in Christ. The old being was sick, unfulfilled, unhappy, and divided. But how can we describe the new being? Jesus said that if the Son shall set you free, you shall be free indeed. Not free to do your own thing, but free under the Lordship of Christ. When you give up control of your life, you have a new kind of freedom. You lose the tyranny of other people and their opinions. The new being is whole. The word *salvation* means "whole or well" and encompasses both physical and spiritual wellness.

Another goal we should be aiming at in one-to-one counseling is to enable the other person to experience the fruits of the Spirit: joy, peace, patience, goodness, gentleness. We can expect God to bring these about, in us and through us. But there is no one way to wholeness—one standard answer. There are as many reasons for and forms of sickness as there are individuals. We need to find where the other person is and begin to relate that person to what God is offering.

A medical doctor has no one prescription for all ailments and neither did Jesus. A rich young ruler came; he was talented, privileged. He had everything but something was missing. Jesus said to him, "Sell all that you have and follow me." He said that only once to one person. He was saying, "Here is My prescription for you." To the woman caught in adultery, He said, "I don't condemn you. Go and sin no more." Those are hard words—go and sin no more. He said that one time to one person. Nicodemus, theologian, Pharisee, and a very ethical and moral man, came saying, "What is this Kingdom of God you were talking about? How do I find it?" Jesus said to this proud and wise man, "You've got to let go of that pride and be born again." He said that once to one person—"You've got to be born again"—and apparently Nicodemus was, because later on, when all the diciples forsook Jesus, he claimed His body.

Jesus wrote a different prescription for each person. If you have to learn all the prescriptions from some book, you're not in the ballpark. In one-to-one encounters, the point is to try to determine what God is saying about that particular person's stuck point and the route they might take to find life and wholeness.

We are not called to give rules to people, but to love people into finding a source of love. The church for years has been stuck on what the Roman Catholics call "moral theology." Years ago, when the Roman church was much less flexible, there were volumes on moral theology. You could consult a priest and say, "This is my problem. What shall I do?" And then he could find the answer for you in one of those volumes. There was a rule for everything. We Protestants don't have a set of volumes, but we still have some rigid rules.

In seminary the professor who frustrated me most was the man I later most appreciated. I went to seminary as an evangelical, and there were many just like me at Princeton. We wanted our professors to tell us clearly the right and the wrong. We wanted answers to the really important questions, such as: Can Christians smoke? Can Christians drink? Can Christians dance? Those very questions date me. He said, "I won't give you answers, and I hope you won't give answers to those who come to you for counseling. They'll want you to tell them what to do in every situation. You do that, and you'll fail them." We said, "Ah, typical liberal. He's hedging. He doesn't know the answers. He doesn't know God's will about these things."

About five or six years later, I revisited the seminary and thanked that professor. I finally understood what he was trying to communicate—that the ultimate issue is a person's relationship to God. The presenting problem, for example, "My marriage is failing" or "I drink too much" is a means of helping that person understand where they are in this basic relationship. To provide an answer to their problem, even if it is a good answer, is to fail them. In any one-to-one counseling situation, remember that you are aiming at something bigger than an answer to a temporary problem.

Resources

Our primary resource for counseling—yours and mine— is the Holy Spirit himself. He is the person whose presence makes this one-to-one counseling effective, because He is concerned about and involved with every person you meet. So when you sit down with someone, stranger or friend, you are not alone. There is a triangle there. There is you and the other person and there is someone else who cares far more about that person than you do, God's own Spirit. That Spirit has access to the unconscious. The Spirit is the ultimate resource, and you and I need only cooperate with Him. He will do the work if we are vulnerable and pay the price and don't get in the way. We have a resource beyond our own wisdom. In medicine, doctors know they don't actually heal anybody. They have said that while they change the bandages, God heals the wounds. Sometimes in Christian counseling we think that our cleverness gets results. Effective counseling does not depend on our smarts and our wisdom.

Your second resource is your faith in Jesus Christ. It's your faith that gives you hope. If you have hope for yourself when you sit down with somebody who is lost, wandering, sunk, depressed, or guilty, you can have hope for them. Hope is the result of the fact that there is somebody in your life who loves you unconditionally, irrevocably, and forever and ever. You're home free.

A third resource in effective one-to-one counseling is your belief in the strength and integrity of the other person. This can be difficult. You may be dealing with somebody who has failed repeatedly, and it's hard to believe they have any strength or integrity. Our youngest son is a probation officer. One of his parolees is a seventeen-year-old boy who has been arrested for burglary about a dozen times. While he was on probation, he committed five more burglaries. Society would say there is no hope for that boy. Our son says, "I tell him about me when I was a hopeless case, when I was in trouble. If enough people around him believe in him as they did in me, maybe he can make it after all." There are no hopeless cases. There is something of God in that person that you may be able to call forth.

The Genuine Helper

Let's talk now about some of the characteristics of the genuine helper that we can develop to do effective one-to-one counseling, to be people whom God can use to help somebody else in a stuck place.

1. First of all, the effective counselor is a fellow struggler, not a know-it-all. We read in Acts 14:14 that the apostles performed a miracle, and the crowd was so impressed they wanted to offer sacrifices to them. When Barnabas and Paul heard about these plans, they tore their clothes and ran into the middle of the crowd, saying, "What are you doing? Why are you doing this? We're just men, human beings like you." The apostles who were filled with the Holy Spirit were saying, "Listen, we are not magicians. We're just people like you—people in whom there is power, power we want to share with you."

2. The genuine helper is unselfish with his or her time. They are interruptible. No one has enough time. You can be totally occupied just taking care of your house and garden, getting your car serviced, and balancing your checkbook. Whether you are the President of the United States or retired with a staff of servants, the mechanics of living can be all-consuming. There really is no such thing as "spare" time.

So when someone asks, "Do you have a minute?" (which means two or three hours) we could all legitimately say no. But the helper says yes.

Jesus was interruptible. He repeatedly interrupted whatever He was doing to stop and listen. That's a big price to pay. When somebody gives you that kind of time, you suddenly feel loved. They are giving you a piece of their life, because they can't replace those lost hours. It is a very precious commodity. That's why counseling is not easy. Even if you set up a schedule to see people, you may be called at any hour and you may find you need to be interruptible. That's what communicates love.

3. The genuine helper does not give sympathy. Jesus did not give sympathy. I don't know of a single instance in the Gospels where He sat down with someone in trouble, sick, possessed of demons, immoral, or whatever and said, "You poor thing." He wept with those going to funerals and he laughed with those going to weddings. He empathized rather than sympathized. We have often equated love with sympathy. But sympathy is usually patronizing and enfeebling. Sympathy implies, "Ain't it awful? You're brave to put up with that. That's the best you are capable of." Love says, "I believe you can come through this situation." Love asks tough questions. Love doesn't settle for the mess the other person is in.

Sympathy is addictive. Those who are hooked on it can't get enough. They go from one to another in the church saying, "My husband is still drinking. My kid is still on pot. My arthritis is worse than ever." They enjoy the sympathy so much there is no incentive to change the situation. Like Jesus we are to weep with those who weep, laugh with those who laugh. But let's be very careful about giving sympathy.

I have said before that I believe there are no victims in relationships. Very few of the people I counsel, professionally or just incidentally, come to complain about their health or their finances. Mostly they are caught in some unfulfilling relationship. Somebody isn't giving them enough of or the right kind of love, attention, or support. They are having problems with a husband, wife, child, friend, boss. Hard as it sounds, anybody who is suffering because of a relationship has allowed that to happen. They have given the other person the power to hurt them.

4. The genuine helper does not always enjoy helping or counseling. I am a little suspicious of people who like or enjoy counseling. The best counselors I know have confessed to me that they would prefer never again to see anybody one to one. It's too costly, too hard. It demands too much. If somebody calls you at two o'clock in the morning asking for help, you need not be thrilled to have them call you. You might say, "Well, come on over. I'll put the coffeepot on." Or you might ask, "Can it wait until morning? I'll see you at eight o'clock in the morning." Whatever you do, don't feel guilty about not being thrilled. Whether you're thrilled or not, God is there. If you will not pretend you feel good about it but simply be available and believe again that there is a third person present in God's own Spirit, miracles can happen.

We read that Jesus was touched by someone in the crowd,

a woman who was instantly healed of a disease she had endured for years. And though there were thousands pressing around him, he said, "Somebody touched me." He felt power go out of him. If you really are involved in caring for people, you'll feel power go out of you. You're going to be tired when you're done. Simply being there and being a partner with the Spirit, listening and caring and doing the things that we're talking about, is hard work.

Specifics

To sum it up, we are talking about being there and being real. We are talking about believing that every counseling situation is a triangular relationship with you, the other person, and the Holy Spirit. Beyond that, how can we help people with specifics?

Meaning

Though the presenting symptoms are job or marriage, it may be that the real problem is the need for a whole new center to a life. You may be called on to help the other person find their life in the Kingdom with the King at the center. This is not the time to attempt a short course on Christianity, the incarnation, the atonement, the second coming. Accepting Christ is not saying true or false to the concept of a saviour. We want to help people say yes to the person of

God Himself. And before they know the marvelous doctrines and understand who Jesus is, they can say yes to the Person who is the center of the universe.

An old friend of mine in Philadelphia is a chemist with a Ph.D. He became a Christian and tried to live it out on the job. One day, a co-worker came over for lunch. He said, "Ed, I really see a change in you. There is a joy and a peace and a quietness you never had before. I wish I could have that." Ed said, "I have become a Christian and you can do that too." The friend was skeptical. "Well, my background is Unitarian and I don't know much about this whole thing. I'd like to make the kind of commitment you have. I'm just not sure I believe in Jesus Christ." With a flash of God-given wisdom, Ed said, "Well, can you make a turnip?" "Certainly not" was the answer. "I'm only a chemist." "I can't make one either," said Ed. "Do you think you can turn your life over to the Great Turnipmaker?" Yes, I could do that," was the reply. And he actually prayed, "Great Turnipmaker, I give you my life." A relationship began, for among other things, Jesus is the Great Turnipmaker. Ed put the concept of Jesus in terms meaningful to a chemist. In a matter of weeks he knew Jesus as far more than the Great Turnipmaker.

The effective one-to-one counselor will not take anyone for granted. I have met evangelical church members who have confessed that they have never met *the* Person, and they really would like to. In one-to-one counseling, don't be afraid to ask if they want to make that decision. Don't be

afraid of pressure. Nobody can be pressured into the Kingdom unwillingly.

Guilt

In one-to-one counseling you will see a good many people
who are trying to deal with guilt. They may be Christians
who said yes to the Lord, but are doing something harmful
and destructive to themselves or to others. We Christians
have the only answer for guilt. Humanistic psychology and
psychiatry and the behavioral sciences have no answers.
They can help you with guilt feelings, those vague feelings
of "dis-ease" which are the result of not meeting expectations laid on you by parents, church, society, or yourself.
You are not perfect and you have failed. But real guilt is a
result of having failed yourself and God, of having hurt
people around you. The secular world has no remedy for
that. I've been at Gestalt-therapy workshops where most of
the participants are wrestling with real guilt. They are physically ill because they have done something bad and they
know it.

We Christians take guilt seriously. A woman came to see
me about a year ago and said, "I love my husband, but I
have had an affair. I feel terrible about it. I have already
been to a psychiatrist and counselor and they both said to
forget it—nobody's perfect. What do you think?" I said, "I
think you've done a terrible thing. If you love your husband
and he trusted you and you had an affair, that's a terrible
thing." She said, "You mean it's OK to feel bad?" I said,

"That's the way you ought to feel. That's the starting point for forgiveness and healing. The good news is that you're forgiven if you want to be." So when you counsel people, honor their guilt. God's spirit produced it. We can walk away from our sins after we admit them because Christ has paid the price.

Change can occur at the point where we stop making excuses for our behavior. This is the premise of a new thrust in dealing with those labeled "criminally insane." The effectiveness of such labeling is being questioned. If the diagnosis is "criminally insane," that's an illness with no known cure. We're being told that it's more helpful to go on the premise that the offender has willfully chosen to commit a crime. If we've done something bad we can be rehabilitated. If someone is labeled "insane," he can be warehoused forever. The hardness of God is kinder than the softness of men. We have sentimentally believed that no one in their right mind could have done such a "bad" thing. If we're allowed to own up to those bad things, we can change our behavior.

Direction

In any one-to-one counseling situation you're going to be called upon to help people make decisions about the direction of their life. You'll be asked to help them sort out values and priorities—what's important and in what order—money, power, relationships. Each of us has our hierarchy of values. Those who don't know their own hierarchy of values are always confused. "Shall I take this job,

marry this person, join that committee, buy this house?"
Most of us who are counselors are tempted to impose our
own value system on the other person. But it's more helpful
to encourage that other person to find his or her own. You
need to keep asking, "What is most important to you?" In
premarital counseling, I try to help couples become aware of
their individual values. If money, success, and career are
important to one and the other wants lots of freedom and
leisure, they're on a collision course. As they trade their life
inch by inch every day, make sure they are trading it for
those things that they really want. Does the person they plan
to marry share their goals and values?

When someone is stuck in terms of direction, brainstorm
together all the possible courses of action. Let's say he or she
is caught in an unrewarding job. What are the options? He
can quit his job. He can try to communicate his feelings to
the boss. He can bide his time and send out a résumé. He
can list some things he'd really *like* to do. This kind of
brainstorming can produce wisdom and insight.

Depression

Perhaps one of the most common presenting symptoms in
any couseling situation is depression. You are going to see
people who feel rotten, discouraged, inferior, full of self-
hate. The new psychiatry is giving us some wonderful new
insights into treating this kind of problem. Many psychiatrists believe, contrary to classical Freudians, that it is easier
to act your way into new feelings than to feel your way into

new actions. Freud would say that depression is the result of feelings of no worth. These stem from your early childhood experiences, pre and postnatal. As you relive those feelings on the couch and work them through, you feel better about yourself and will eventually perform better. The new school of psychiatry says you have no control over your feelings, but you *do* over your actions. You feel depressed because you're not acting responsibly. When you start behaving responsibly, even in small things, your feelings about yourself will change. People who are unable to control how they feel can begin to do those things that make them feel better.

To sum up, I would like to suggest some things to keep in mind in every one-to-one situation. First, enjoy the person if you can. That's not possible with everybody. Some people you will just endure. But if it is possible, there is no greater gift you can give than to enjoy being with him or her. People hate to be projects. I can't think of anybody Jesus spent time with who felt they were His project.

Next, ask caring, sensitive questions and listen aggressively to the answers. Listening is such an important part of any one-to-one counseling situation that I will deal with it separately in the next chapter.

React honestly to what is being said. If something sounds outrageous, you can say so. Love takes the person seriously. Love is demanding. Love is real. It's not mushy and it's not spiritual. Let the Spirit make you a real person in the relationship, not some spiritual type.

I did a premarital counseling session a few months ago. In the course of the session it became obvious that the prospec-

tive bridegroom was very hostile. Since I had worked them
into a very busy schedule, I found myself reacting to him.
After about a half hour, I said to the prospective bride,
"Listen, I think you're in big trouble if you marry this guy.
Here I am, a stranger to both of you, really. I'm giving you
time and I'm getting nothing but guff from him. If he treats
me, a stranger doing him a favor, that way, how's he going
to treat you?" Needless to say they were both visibly
shocked. At that, the man said, "Can I talk to you alone?"
When the woman left, he began, with some tears, to share
some of his problems. This kind of confrontative style is new
to me. Years ago I would have been polite and ignored his
rudeness. But when I finally said, "What in thunder are you
being so rude about?" we got to the stuck place in his life.
He apologized to his fiancee and to me. Instead of playing some game, I am becoming more free to say, "What are
you doing and why?"

Believe that God can use whatever you are at the moment. When somebody knocks on your door at midnight or
stops you in the hall or asks unexpectedly for a piece of your
time, it isn't your choice. It's really like emergency surgery.
A doctor, called at 2 A.M., may be tired or irritated or depressed, but he responds anyway. If he is a Christian, he
says, "God, use my hands to help this person who has been
in an accident." You and I are called in for surgery of the
soul, and that's often emergency surgery.

Ask if there is anything he or she has never told anybody.
This is a powerful question to use, particularly with someone who is depressed. If they say yes, you can suggest that

you are available. The Bible tells us God heals if we confess
our sins to one another. He is faithful and just to forgive. We
are already forgiven, but the cleansing comes with the confession. The Roman church has kept this tradition alive for
two thousand years. We Protestants scorned person-to-per-
son confession, and modern psychiatry flourished. We sit on
our secrets. We are crippled, not by our sins but by our con-
cealment.

Finally, pray for and with the other person. If they have
made an appointment in advance, pray before the appointment. If you are caught unexpectedly in a counseling situation, then pray silently at that moment. Be aware of the
triangular relationship. Pray positively. Don't pray picturing
their problem and their sad face. Pray visualizing them as
you think God meant them to be. Claim what you believe
God has in mind for that person. And then, pray with the
other person. Pray whatever prayer is appropriate. You may
want to have a laying on of hands for a physical or psychic
problem. You may have to have a "funeral" to bury hurtful
memories or old resentments.

No matter how much modern medicine continues to
amaze us with its enormous hospital complexes and bur-
geoning technology, its effectiveness still hinges on the face-
to-face dialogue between doctor and patient. In the same
way, God's power to transform our lives most often depends
on our capacities as believers to enter into meaningful face-
to-face relationships with one other person. That's where the
high adventure begins.

12

Giving Yourself Away— In Aggressive Listening

The major part of most of our lives is spent in relationships. That's why there is nothing more important than to find ways to improve those relationships. In these next pages I'd like to talk about some of our behaviors and attitudes that tend either to block or enhance relationships. We can have a relationship at any number of different levels. Let's begin with what I consider the least effective level, that of indifference. To be treated with indifference means that you are ignored. Nobody pays any attention to you. There is no hostility. You are simply overlooked. I think indifference is the most destructive level of relationship. Hell is full of people who are indifferent. They are bored by God and by each other. They are totally self-absorbed. In *The Great Divorce*, C. S. Lewis gives us a picture of hell as a city where people who can't stand each other have moved farther and farther away, and the town limits are being continually extended.

The next level of relationship is one in which you are being continually criticized. That's better than being ignored. You must have some worth if people are always picking on you, straightening you out, giving you advice. They at least take you seriously.

Then there is the next level of relationship, where one party is the advice giver. There are a lot of people out there eager to tell you how to live your life, what to wear, what to say, what to do, how to behave, and what to think. Sometimes this is done in the guise of witnessing. It is witnessing that implies, "Let me tell you what I've done that you ought to do." It's not all bad. Some of us are Christians because of this kind of witnessing.

But even more effective witnessing takes place at the next level of relationship, where you are giving tangible help. This is incarnational love. You are not just telling people God loves them. You are Jesus on two legs, being there and helping somebody—with their income tax, driving somebody to the hospital, loaning money, putting somebody up on your hide-a-bed overnight. This is the level at which you are really communicating that the other person is of worth. You are giving a piece of yourself when you give your time, money, and energy. It's hard to measure what that does for people.

But an even higher level of relationship is one in which you can ask for help. A lot of people are programmed to give help, but it's hard to ask for it. In so many of Jesus' relationships recorded in the Gospels, we find Him receiving help. In His three years of ministry He is at the mercy of the hospitality of friends. He asks Zacchaeus for food, the Samaritan woman for water. He asks the disciples for their company in the Garden of Gethsemane. He said and says, "I need you." It is at this point we discover what vulnerability is. We are vulnerable when we let somebody else know we have needs and that they can help us.

I was talking to a man recently who told me an interesting story of how he became a Christian. A few years ago he was in Victoria, British Columbia, on a holiday. He went to a store that sold souvenirs. Nobody else was in there except for a lady behind the cash register. He had been browsing around for three or four minutes when she suddenly said, "Say, would you help me?" He went over and found she was reading a Bible. Pointing to the section she was reading, she said, "What do you think this means?" He read it and told her what he thought it meant. "Thanks," she said, "That's helpful. I was really puzzled." Now to this day he doesn't know whether she was a Christian or not. But through her, God got this man's attention for the first time. Having read that one section, he rushed back to his hotel room and read the Gideon Bible for three hours. Something new began in his life because one lady said, "What do you think this means?"

Most of our witness to people implies that we know something they don't know. We have all seen the bumper stickers that say, "I've found it." I understand their purpose and I agree with it. I'm not as keen about that particular strategy.

It implies, "*I* have found it. Are you so dumb you haven't found it?" Well, if you haven't found it, you are dumb, but who wants to be told that? The ultimate message of the Gospel is that God sent His Son to die for us because we have worth. And if we imply that those who haven't found Him yet are dumb, it reverses that basic message.

At the top of the effectiveness level is the relationship in which listening takes place. A lot of us are in trouble simply because we have never had anyone care enough to really listen to us. Psychologically, they tell us you cannot differentiate aggressive listening from love. Somebody who is a real listener is projecting love whether they feel it or not. If you come into a room and want to find out where love is taking place, look for somebody leaning forward in a conversation, straining to hear what the other person is saying. That's what love would look like. To be listened to is really ultimate affirmation.

Aggressive listening is not the kind of listening confined to "Uh huh." Aggressive listening follows up with sensitive questions—not with nosy questions. Let's say someone confesses to you that they are having an affair. Don't say, "With whom?" and "For how long?" That's not the kind of question I'm talking about. Ask instead, "How do you feel about doing this? Why do you think it began?" When we're in trouble we need someone who can enable us to explore what we are doing and why we are doing it.

The ability to do this kind of listening will be determined largely by our emotional equipment, our genes, our training. Methods vary. Two of the most skilled counselors I know have very different styles. Paul Tournier, Swiss physician, simply loves people and listens to them. He says he doesn't know exactly what he is doing. He has no method, no technique. He just sits down and says, "Tell me." He is a passive person and a passive listener. He is the founder of The Medicine of the Whole Person, in association with many wholistic physicians around the world. One of his closest associates is the German psychiatrist Walther Lechler, mentioned previously. Walther is someone who gets aggressively involved with his patients. I've been to his clinic in the Black Forest, and I've watched him as he deals with people. He wrestles with them and physically pummels them. He yells and shouts and cries. He's involved in their lives. I asked Paul Tournier, "How can you and Walther be in such agreement about the medicine of the whole person? You couldn't be more different." He explained that The Medicine of the Whole Person has nothing to do with being passive or aggressive. The Medicine of the Whole Person simply means taking people seriously and loving them. How you do that depends upon your personality. He said he sends those who need an aggressive counselor to Walther, or someone like him.

If the most effective relationships are those in which aggressive listening takes place, then what are some of the things we should be listening for—some of the handles that can help get people over the stuck places in their lives? Sometimes people are stuck because of secrets—things they have never dared tell anybody. You become your secrets, those things you consciously hold within. If on the other hand, you confess your sins to one another as the Bible says, God by His grace dissipates those sins. If you hide all your good deeds, your alms giving, your all-night praying, your fasting, your generosity, you become those good things. But a lot of us have buried our garbage instead.

All of us are sexual beings and often our secrets are sexual transgressions that we are not free to talk about. Recent studies in the United States indicate that four out of every ten children are somehow sexually abused at some time in their lives. At least one out of every ten is abused by a parent or relative. Now if we are never able to talk about this, the abused party feels unclean and cut off from the rest of society. They are being destroyed not by the bad thing that happened, which is certainly horrible, but by the fear and guilt of having a shameful secret. So listen for secrets. If people feel love they may be able to tell you something they have never told anyone before. Do the kind of listening that will enable an honest confession. The word *confession* sounds so liturgical, but it is simply telling someone else the bad thing that happened to us or the bad thing that we did.

Listen for fears. Fears paralyze people. Listen for the person who is afraid of being afraid, who fears failure. You can tell them that part of the Good News is that failure is OK. You won't find the word *success* in the Bible. And God teaches us best through our failures. If you believe you must not fail, you are spiritually catatonic. Encourage the other person to talk about his or her fears.

I met a woman recently at a conference who told me about her psychiatrist, an unusually caring and creative person. For a long time she had been terrified about life in general and particularly about driving a car. She was afraid to go more than a block from home. She couldn't do the shopping. She was really handicapped. Her psychiatrist suggested they go out and try driving. She said, "You're afraid to go more than a block from your house. We'll get in the car and go two blocks and see how it feels. Then we'll try three blocks." She was finally driving for miles and finding it was not so scary after all.

It seems this same psychiatrist had another patient, whose problem was a lack of self-worth. She hadn't bought herself any clothes in years because she didn't feel she was worth it. Her husband was successful and well-to-do. She went around looking grungy. Her doctor suggested they go shopping together and helped her buy some new clothes, which are contributing to a new self-image. This is a whole new age of medicine we are in, where some doctors are helping people by becoming involved in personal and practical ways. Now you may need psychiatric training to attempt to treat some serious mental illness, but you and I are equipped to help people with concrete fears and to do what this caring psychiatrist did.

Listen for loneliness. Loneliness is not aloneness. Loneliness comes from broken relationships or unrewarding relationships or no relationships. As we said earlier, it is the number-one killer in America according to medical research out of Johns Hopkins University. Loneliness causes many cardiovascular and cancer deaths. People are ashamed to be alone or to seem lonely. And yet loneliness is one of God's gifts. It drives us to intimacy. If I share my loneliness with you, I give you the gift of love and that results in community. If I conceal my loneliness, I am cut off and it increases.

Listen for pain. Listen for the pain people are in right now—a physical, psychological, emotional pain that is a result of their failures. In our society, bars provide an outlet for people in pain. Most people in bars are not alcoholics; the alcoholic is generally a solitary drinker. Bars are peopled by ordinary citizens who want to sit and talk about their pain without being judged. If you can help someone talk about his or her pain, they may begin to deal with it constructively.

Those are some of the negative things to listen for. But we need to train ourselves to listen for the positive as well. Our listening can help someone begin to discover the wealth that God has put into their lives. Most people are living on one-tenth of their spiritual resources. Help them mine the gold in their lives. Listen for gifts—gifts of which people are often unaware. We all know our talents and skills, but it is harder to recognize the gifts that we have. God has buried gifts in everybody. But until somebody cares enough to look for our gifts, we'll never find them. Most of us take jobs in life based upon our skills, and these may be one-tenth of our capacity and capability. The fun begins when you work in the area of your gifts. Effectiveness is multiplied.

A pastor friend of mine told me about a man who was a new convert in his church. He came to ask if the pastor had any particular job for him. Though he seemed to have no obvious skill that the organized church could use, the pastor said he'd pray about it. Eventually he forgot the request. A year later he got an invitation from this same man to give the invocation at a banquet for his Boy Scout troop. He went and found his parishioner had become scoutmaster for a blind, retarded Boy Scout troop. It seems he even organized a special group for overnight camp-outs. They would join up with a regular troop and pair up one-to-one and go off camping. Those kids were coming alive because of their leader's gifts for doing something which, probably, nobody else in that town had thought of.

The church is in the habit of using people in the area of their skills. We ask teachers to teach in the church school, business people to serve on the stewardship committee, builders to oversee the property. We have got to get beyond that and help each other find gifts.

Listen for strengths. Most people are not aware of their strengths. They are all too aware of their failures. Listen to dreams and hopes. Listen to interests. Listen to history. Ask the other person about his or her family, not just the present one, but the one he grew up with. Those things that happened ten, twenty, or even fifty years ago have produced the person you see now. What happened around that dining room table with parents, or no parents, or siblings, has shaped us all and we are still those children.

Aggressive listening is far from easy. That's probably why it is so rare. Listening that takes people seriously is taxing. Pray as you do it. Say, "Lord, I am a weak person. I bore easily. This is not going to be fun. It may be dull. But it's important." In a one-to-one relationship you may say,

"Lord, I'm tired, my mind is wandering, right now I want to hear this person. It's hard work. Give me Your grace that I can become an aggressive listener."

Relating at this level can initiate a friendship that lasts for life. In the old days in China, if you happened to save someone's life, they became your devoted slave. You couldn't get rid of them. They lived in your house because you owned them. There is a parallel for us. When you start helping someone, you may end up owning them, at least emotionally. If you begin to really care for somebody, for the first time or the one hundredth time, you'll pay a price. You can't say, "Don't call me, I'll call you." They'll call you and they'll be back. That's probably why we don't get involved in this kind of listening more than we do. It's costly. There is no safe place.

Love doesn't give advice. Love doesn't tell the other person to shape up. We can trust the Holy Spirit to speak to that person and give direction. You might say, "What do you think you ought to do?" If you're talking to a Christian, you can even say, "What do you think God is telling you to do?" Let the other person tell you what he or she thinks God or the inner voice is saying. And hold them to that—to the thing *they* ought to do.

As a listener, insist that the other person deal with reality. Don't allow them to play games. I had a relative by marriage who was always trying to win her mother-in-law's approval. The mother-in-law despised her, and for some concrete reasons. She is an alcoholic and somewhat disturbed. But this woman calls me frequently and reviews all the rotten things her mother-in-law has done to her. And she always ends the conversation by saying, "But you know, she really loves me." I say, "No, dear, she doesn't love you. She may never love you. And you have to make peace with that." I refuse to buy into her fantasy.

An effective listener gets people to take responsibility for their lives. There are no victims, as I have said before, at least relationally. There are no strong and weak types. Paul Tournier, in his book on the strong and the weak, says the strong shout, yell, bully, and threaten, while the weak get their way by other means—withholding, sulking, being moody. But the point is, everybody has a way of exerting power. Don't allow a person to pretend to be an innocent victim in a relationship. Whatever the situation, they have allowed it to happen. They have other choices. Help them to take responsibility for their lives and their choices.

When you're listening to somebody, your differences and your similarities can both be of help in building a relationship. If their background and experience is similar to yours, you can say, "I think I know how you feel . . . that happened to me too." If they have done something totally out of the realm of your experience, you can express interest and get them to tell you about it.

Let's remember that Jesus was an aggressive listener. We are aware of that as we read the accounts of the many encounters He had with various people. He listened to the man by the pool. He listened as the invalid complained about the people who had failed him. What happened after that? There may have been an hour of dialogue—who knows? But

Jesus finally said, "You are healed." Jesus listened to the
Gerasene demoniac, a crazy psychotic man who was living
in a cemetery up in the hills where he could bother no one.
He came running to meet Jesus and his first words were,
"Leave me alone." We all have friends like that. They may
say, "Quit bugging me about the church," when actually we
haven't said a word. They say, "I can't believe in this Jesus
stuff," but somehow they're always hanging around. In this
encounter, Jesus asks the question "What is your name?"
"My name is Legion, for we are many," was the answer.
What do you suppose Jesus said after that? "Tell me some of
your names? How did you get all those names? What name
do you like the best? What name do you wish you had? Who
are you?" We don't know how long the encounter actually
took, but finally the demons left the man, and the townspeo-
ple came out to find him clothed and in his right mind. (*See*
Mark 5:1-15.)

We humans are not basically chemicals and atoms. Basically we are an idea of God, but we've gone astray. Something destructive has happened. We're in a stuck place and
we're standing on the hose of God's grace. Jesus modeled
effective dialogue for us. And if we can learn to be effective
listeners, we can channel the grace of God to other people
and bring hope and healing.

13

You and the Household of God

The next time you go to church, look around you and see who's there. Look at the strange assortment of people who are sitting beside you, around you, in front of, and behind you. I suggest you'll find you are sitting in the middle of a mystery. There is no way to explain why that particular congregation has come together. Who are they? Why are they there and what does it all mean?

Some day I'd like to take a tape recorder and go out on the busy street near our church and interview people, asking them to tell me in twenty-five words or less what they think about the church—our particular church. It would be fascinating to discover how people out there see us: those members of other churches, nonbelievers, atheists, freethinkers.

How do our neighbors, average citizens, see us? Who
are we?

Carlyle Marney, recently deceased Baptist preacher and
writer, spoke to this question.

> What's in the church? Ask people out there, our neighbors
> and friends, and you get a variety of answers. An easy
> touch is in there, says the professional transient. A neces-
> sary superstition is in there, says an anthropologist, who
> knows only that all cultures support these quaint beliefs.
> A fine political ally is in there, says Constantine and most
> emperors and all governors, except the one who called the
> Little Rock Christians names, not knowing he would need
> them later on. What's in there? A tie with our sacred past,
> says the ancestor worshipper, whether Shintoist or DAR.
> A mighty fine preserver of the status quo is in there, says
> the social conservative who fears all change. The church is
> a harmless and mildy beneficent cathartic, says the psy-
> chologist. A convenient January or April charity, says the
> economic opportunist.

These may all be ways in which the world sees us, but
what about the professional theologians who are trying to
probe the mystery of the Body of Christ? Who do they say
we are? Back in the sixteenth century when we Protestants
emerged as another part of the Body of Christ, Reformed
theologians set down certain guidelines.

They believed, first of all, that where the word of God is
preached and the sacraments are distributed—there is the

church. Further, they believed the church, the Body of Christ, to be both sinful and holy because its members are both sinful and holy. Within this church, which depends solely on the Holy Spirit for its life and direction, the ministry is to be shared by both the clergy and the laity, who make up a priesthood of believers.

One of our wisest theologians of a century ago, Charles Hodge, said, "Our unity as the Body of Christ cannot be applied to any promiscuous mass of saints, be it Reformed, Protestant, Catholic, Evangelical, Orthodox." If so, then how would you describe the church? What is the source of our unity in this church to which most of us belong and have given our allegiance? Certainly, we are not a people who are in political agreement. In the early sixties, my wife and I had some faithful friends, people who had been with us through dark times and good times. Suddenly we found ourselves on opposite sides of the chaotic political situation of the sixties. My wife and I said, "How can our brother and sister in Christ see this so differently than we do?" How can this be? Recently, a parishioner handed me a quote that speaks to this, "How am I supposed to fly like an eagle when I'm cooped up with a bunch of turkeys?" Most of us have wondered at some time how we got yoked with people who do not see things our way. We know what's right and true, and we're stuck with this bunch of turkeys who are blind to such clear revelation.

It blows our minds that people who are brothers and sisters in Christ can be so diverse in some of the most basic

things. Next time you go to church, look around you sur-
reptitiously. You'll see some members of your congregation
who have been known to follow the biblical injunction to
take a little wine for the stomach. There are others there
who would not be caught dead taking a drop of alcohol.
You'll see some extreme right-wing Republicans and some
left-wing Democrats. In my own congregation there are
people who have the simplest kind of life-style. They have
given up owning a car and get around on public transporta-
tion in order to give more money to missions. Others drive
gas guzzlers. Can one congregation hold two such opposing
points of view?

Then there are the premillennialists and the post-
millennialists and those who don't know what that all
means. Some members of the congregation say that the first
item on the church's agenda is missions, especially foreign
missions. Others want to concentrate on their own city and
country and clean up the mess there. There are people who
are tithers several times over. Some are still token givers and
have no sense of partnership with God. Some members
would prefer to have the choir sing only the great old clas-
sics. They hate anything contemporary. Others say, "The
new stuff is the best music of all." It seems we can have di-
vergent musical views and still be one. Some members are
suspect because of their vocation. They are asked how they
can call themselves Christian and be in some particular
business. The answer could be, "It's easy. I'm serving Christ
in this place."

What all of this says, it seems to me, is that you had better beware of making your theological, ethical, moral, political, and social views the criteria for unity. Taken to its logical conclusion, you'll end up in a church of one person—you. Nobody else will quite fit your definition of a Christian. What does the Bible have to say about all this? In Isaiah, we read what God says to Israel, the people of the Old Covenant. "Fear not, for I have redeemed you. I have called you by name. You are mine and everyone who is called by My name whom I created for My glory and whom I formed and made, I have made you one" (*see* Isaiah 43:1, 7). And then we find Paul writing in Ephesians, "So then you are no longer strangers and sojourners, but you are fellow citizens with the saints and members of the household of God" (2:19 RSV).

That is the mystery of who we are. Somehow God Himself has said to us, "You are now a part of a family of which I and my Son and my Spirit are the head. You are members of my family." It's a mystery and our unity is in one thing only—it is in Jesus Christ Himself. There is no other logical basis for our unity. We are one because of Jesus Christ, His life, His death, His resurrection, His presence with us in worship. He has chosen us, He has called us by name, He has given His life for us. As we come to Him, He gives us to each other. He says, "Look around you, this weird bunch of people you worship with are members of the household also." You may say, "But they don't believe quite as I do." He says, "That's not your problem. You belong to Me now and this is my house." It is the mystery of a family.

If you are in a family with more than one child, you know

the mystery of a household—no two are alike. Some members of the household see God as a mighty healer. Others see him as a source of social justice to deliver the oppressed. Some see God as a source of wisdom. Their faith centers in reading and studying. Because of who we are, we come to God with different needs. God supplies those needs and somehow, though different, we are one household.

The mark of being in a household is that you are loved and accepted. You come just as you are and you are loved and forgiven. Many years ago I led a retreat for a church in the Middle West. On this three-day retreat, I kept hearing about one church member who had touched so many lives by the contagion of her own witness and reality of her love. She was now dying of cancer. She came to the retreat with a great bandage over half of her face because the disease had caused the loss of an eye and part of her face. I finally got to meet her, and I was able to tell her about the many people I had met whose lives had been touched and blessed by her love and prayers. As we were about to go home, she took me aside and asked a favor. She said, "May I show you what I look like under this bandage?" I said, "I think so." We were alone, off in a dark corner, and she took off her bandage, and there was just nothing there. After about fifteen seconds she put her bandage back on, and she hugged me and said, "Thank you. I needed somebody to see me as I am and love me."

This is what the Body of Christ is, the household of God. We are all crippled. We come with our deformities, failures, ailments, and illnesses. We can begin to reveal to each other who we are. Nobody has it made. And what do we say? Not that we are lovers, but that we are loved. We are members of God's household. Because we believe, we belong.